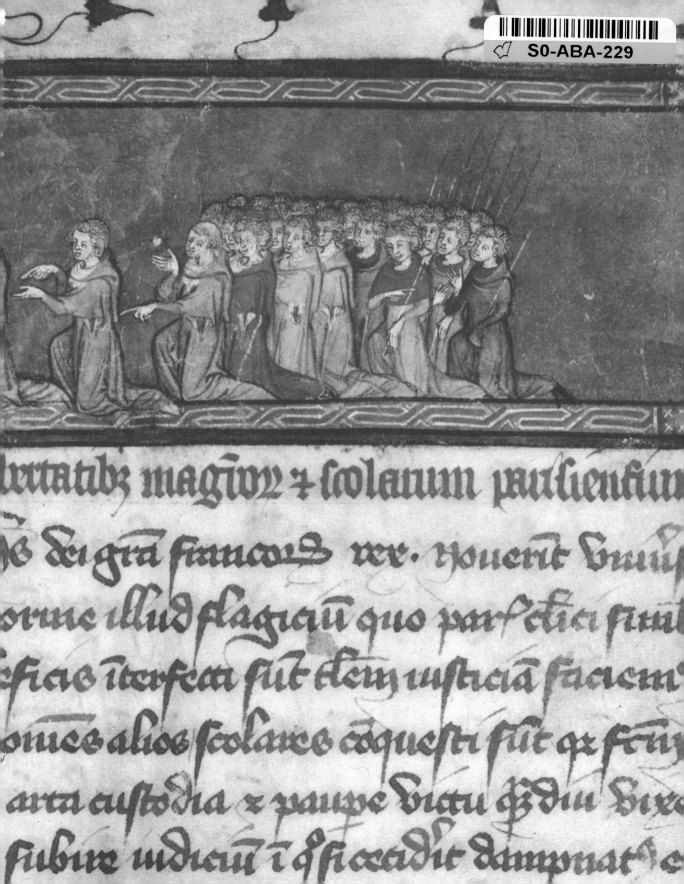

rtatib; magiox̃ ⁊ scolaum parlienkiu

ıo̅ dei gr̃a francoꝛ rex. ꝛouerı̅t br̃uĩ
ornc illud flagız̃qu̅ quo parscliz̃ fıu̅lı
fız̃ıc̅o ı̅terfcci̅ fuit̅ clcꝛy ıuſtıciı̅ faciı̅
onco alıoſ ſcolarco c̃quuſti fuıt oz̃ fcı̅z
arta cuſtodıa ⁊ paupe bıctu cz̃ dıu bıxc
fubıre ıudıciı̅ ı c̃ſi occ̃dıt dãpnat̅

KINGS & QUEENS
OF THE MEDIEVAL WORLD

KINGS & QUEENS
OF THE MEDIEVAL WORLD

FROM WARRIORS AND SAINTS TO PERSECUTORS AND EXILES

MARTIN J. DOUGHERTY

amber
BOOKS

Published by
Amber Books Ltd
United House
North Road
London
N7 9DP
United Kingdom
www.amberbooks.co.uk
Appstore: itunes.com/apps/amberbooksltd
Facebook: www.facebook.com/amberbooks
Twitter: @amberbooks

ISBN: 978-1-78274-642-3

Project Editor: Sarah Uttridge
Designer: Zoe Mellors
Picture Research: Terry Forshaw

Printed in China

1 4 6 8 10 9 7 5 3 2

Contents

INTRODUCTION

The period between the eclipse of the Roman Empire and the beginnings of modern Europe in the Renaissance is known as the medieval period, or Middle Ages. It was a time of great upheaval, with advances in technology and scholarship as well as enormous social changes that would ultimately lead to the rise of the modern nation-state.

THE ROMAN Empire reached its greatest extent in the early years of the second century, creating an era of relative stability in Europe. There was conflict, of course, but commonality of culture and language – along with the threat of military force if stability were threatened – created a veneer of unity. Beneath the surface, however, there were still great differences between the peoples of Europe, and as the Western Roman Empire declined these became ever more obvious.

The westward advance of the Huns in the late fourth century coincided with the decline of Roman power, creating threats that Rome simply could not cope with. Not only was there a direct

Opposite: Defeat at the Battle of the Catalaunian Fields in 451 CE brought an end to the Hunnish incursion into Europe. It marked the emergence of the Franks as a major military force.

threat from the Huns themselves, but also tribes displaced from their traditional homes moved westwards, coming into conflict with other tribes and creating secondary crises.

It is telling that the defeat of the Huns at the Catalaunian Fields in 451 CE came at the hands of a joint Romano-Frankish army. No longer were the Franks just another part of the Roman Empire. They were now an allied kingdom with warriors who fought in their own way rather than in the Roman style.

Although the Hunnish threat to Europe was ended soon afterwards, the power of Rome was broken and its importance rapidly declined. The displaced tribes marched and fought their way across Europe in search of new homelands, and 'barbarian' kingdoms began to emerge. The popular image of this era is one of chaos and violence, a 'dark age' that descended after the light of Rome was extinguished. There is some truth in this, but amid the turbulence a new era was dawning.

THE EARLY MIDDLE AGES

Below: Although the Byzantine Empire had its origins as the Eastern Roman Empire, by the Middle Ages the primary arm of its military forces was armoured cavalry rather than the infantry of the Western Roman Empire.

The Early Middle Ages spanned the period from the fifth century to the tenth, and was an era of great change. Some elements of Roman culture remained highly influential, but at the same time traditional organization along tribal lines began to reassert itself. This was a time of small kingdoms led by warrior monarchs who faced constant threats from their rivals.

The rise of the Islamic Caliphates was a severe threat to the Christian kingdoms of southern Europe. The Iberian Peninsula and parts of the Balkans were conquered by Islamic states, and

VÖLKERWANDERUNG

Left: The mass migrations that took place at the end of the Roman era eradicated the existing provinces and laid the foundations for the realms of medieval Europe – and indeed the states of modern times.

THE VÖLKERWANDERUNG, or Migration Period, was triggered by the arrival of the Huns from the East around 375 CE. Displaced from their homelands by the Huns or by other tribes seeking to move away from the invaders, there was a general movement of whole peoples westwards. The declining Roman Empire resisted as best it could, often by offering tribes new lands in return for acting as a buffer against others travelling in the same direction. This met with mixed success.

Some tribes carved out new homelands, which were named after them. By way of example, Lombardy in Italy is named for the Lombards who conquered it – it is their destination, not their place of origin. Likewise, Burgundy is named for the Germanic tribe who settled there, eventually becoming part of the local political landscape as a state rather than a people.

Other tribes integrated with peoples they encountered along the way or made repeated relocations. The Vandals settled in Iberia, but were pushed onwards by continued conflict. They eventually established a kingdom in North Africa with holdings throughout the western Mediterranean.

These migrations blurred the lines of the old Roman provinces and put new names on the map of Europe; names that would become well known as medieval states.

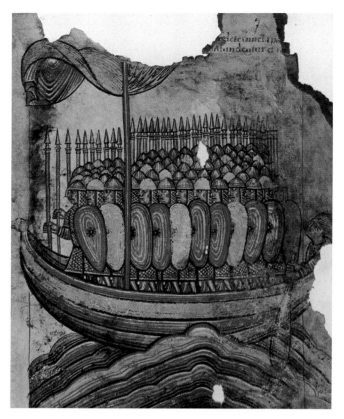

Above: The raids and trading expeditions of the Norsemen were a sufficiently great influence on Europe that the period 793–1066 CE is often known as the 'Viking Era'.

many notable rulers made their name fighting against these incursions. Later, religious fervour would drive Europeans to launch Crusades against the Islamic territories and those of Byzantium, the evolved remnant of the Eastern Roman Empire.

Other threats emerged over time. Scandinavia had been relatively little troubled by the Huns, and, as its population expanded, the people often known as Vikings began to emerge onto the world stage. The term 'Viking' is generally associated with the people of Denmark, Sweden, Norway and Finland, but properly refers only to those engaged in a military or trading expedition. The Scandinavian culture might better be referred to as Norse, but it was the Vikings – those who undertook their great expeditions – that most influenced European history.

Viking expeditions traded along the coasts and up the rivers of Europe, and raided the same areas when this was more profitable. Over time, the raids became larger and were followed by settlement, resulting in Norse kingdoms in England, Northern France, Iceland and even Greenland. The Norsemen also pushed eastwards, into the Slavic lands of what is now Russia. Indeed, Russia gained its name from these people; they were known as the Rus in their new homelands.

The Norse influence on Europe was profound. Resisting their raids forced the emerging kingdoms to evolve and adapt, and in many areas Norse settlers integrated into or overlaid the local culture. In time, the Norsemen became thoroughly European; the Normans who conquered England were Norsemen who had settled along the northern coast of France and become part of Frankish culture.

THE VIKINGS

THE TERM 'Viking' properly applies only to Norsemen engaged in a trading or raiding expedition, but has been applied rather loosely to their entire culture. The Norse people and their expeditions were a major factor in the development of medieval Europe. They did not destroy for the sake of it; Norsemen were happy to trade, farm or settle if that offered a better reward-to-risk ratio than plundering. Similarly, the Viking raiders were not, as some chroniclers suggested, making war on God. Pillaging a monastery was about money, not religion, even though the early Norsemen were pagans.

The adventurous spirit of the Vikings took them down the rivers of Russia to Byzantium, where they traded and were recruited in large numbers into the Varangian Guard. Others sailed around Europe to trade in the Mediterranean, or braved the north Atlantic to found colonies in Iceland and Greenland. A handful even reached North America. In the early medieval period, Viking raids were a constant fear for those who lived on the coast or near a river, but their traders were an important part of the commercial network.

Ultimately, the Norse people evolved medieval kingdoms as 'barbarian' people elsewhere had done. These had differing characters depending on their environment – those who settled in what is now Russia had a quite different culture from the old homelands of Scandinavia or their settlements in Normandy, Ireland and Iceland.

Right: The remains of a 'Viking' settlement were found in 1960 at L'Anse aux Meadows in Newfoundland.

Over time, Roman influences diminished and a feudal system came to dominate politics, with vassals owing allegiance to the next-higher leader in a chain running down from the monarch to the lowliest serf. By the end of the Early Middle Ages, large kingdoms had emerged and elements of modern national identity were beginning to appear.

Right: The primary military force in most kingdoms of the post-Roman period was infantry equipped with a shield and a spear or axe. Cavalry gradually became dominant, with the armoured man-at-arms representing a powerful concentration of mobility and striking power.

Below: The mail shirt or hauberk was the best personal protection available in the Early Middle Ages, though it was later supplanted by articulated plate armour.

THE HIGH MIDDLE AGES

The period from around 1000 CE to 1300 CE is generally known as the High Middle Ages, and was characterized by advancing technology and the rise of powerful kingdoms and empires. Whereas the battlefield had previously been dominated by warriors on foot, the armoured cavalryman was the primary military force of the day. The problem of supporting a professional fighting man – and paying for his extremely expensive equipment – was solved by creating a warrior/ruler class whose upkeep was provided for the most part by their own holdings.

Some professional warriors did exist, paid for by their lord, and contrary to popular belief not all armoured horsemen were noblemen. Commanders and leaders were members of the noble class, but many men-at-arms were commoners who could afford the weapons and equipment required for professional military service. Forces were rounded out by levies of infantry and missile troops such as archers or crossbowmen, often of extremely low quality. Exceptions did exist, such as the yeomen archers of England and the mercenaries who served whatever master could afford their pay, but, overall, infantry were poorly regarded in the High Middle Ages.

This was also an era of castle-building. Fortifications had existed for centuries, of course, but the earth or wooden forts of the Early Middle Ages gradually gave way to increasingly complex stone castles. Warfare typically revolved around either economic damage caused by raiding, or the siege and capture of strong places. The fall of an important castle or fortified town

was not just a military defeat for a monarch; it was a blow to his prestige that might trigger revolts or force hurried negotiations.

Warfare in the Middle Ages has been represented as an unsophisticated brawl between armoured horsemen, with miserable peasants scurrying out of the way. Although not totally inaccurate, this image does not take account of the sophistication that existed at the strategic level. Technical terms existed for several kinds of raid, all of which had definite goals and characteristics. Siege warfare was an advanced art, with many innovative tactics and techniques used to reduce a castle or town. Although this was very much an age of warriors rather than soldiers, their commanders knew their business.

Above: The science of fortification advanced steadily throughout the Middle Ages. Wood and earth castles, typically of a motte and bailey design, were supplanted by advanced stone fortresses in the High Middle Ages.

THE LATE MIDDLE AGES

The Late Middle Ages are generally considered to cover the fourteenth and fifteenth centuries, ending as the Renaissance spread across Europe. The Renaissance was not so much a clearly defined historical era as a cultural movement, which began at different times in different places. Its beginnings were in Italy in the mid-1400s, but England, wracked by the dynastic conflict known as the Wars of the Roses, did not truly embrace the Renaissance until the reign of Elizabeth I, beginning in 1558. By that time, America had been discovered and colonies were being established, and, while some trappings of the medieval era still remained, the world was a very different place.

The Late Middle Ages were characterized by further advances in technology, notably gunpowder. Initially little more than a curiosity, gunpowder allowed the creation of mobile artillery that could pound a previously impregnable castle into ruins. Firearms did not chase the armoured knight off the battlefield, but the social changes that went with them played a part in revolutionizing warfare.

Other technologies were equally important. The creation of ships capable of reliably crossing oceans greatly expanded trade possibilities and allowed the exploration of distant lands. At the same time, religious upheaval was taking place. Protestantism was on the rise, leading to conflicts that were not always fought along national lines. Religious and dynastic wars were often intertwined, as religion was firmly entrenched as part of the national culture, but at times a religious conflict could transcend the borders of kingdoms or even threaten to abolish them.

Enormous social upheaval occurred as a result of the Black Death, which killed such a huge proportion of the European population that labour became a highly valued commodity. No longer did a labourer have to take the wages his master offered; he could walk to another village and get a better deal. The result was a weakening of the power of kings and noblemen and the

Below: The use of gunpowder artillery, albeit of a crude sort, revolutionized siege warfare in the later Middle Ages. Walls that could withstand catapult projectiles were vulnerable to the direct fire of bombards.

rise of a moneyed middle class; factors that allowed the Renaissance to take hold. The feudal system, in which allegiance ran through a hierarchy of nobles, continued to evolve in order to accommodate these changes.

By the end of the Middle Ages, the monarchs of Europe were no longer tribal leaders or warriors who kept their position through force of arms. Clever political machinations were necessary to keep an increasingly powerful nobility from eroding the monarch's power; at the same time, the legitimacy of the ruler was established as much by tradition and dynastic succession as by fitness to lead and ability to defeat enemies. Perhaps not coincidentally, the kings and queens of Europe claimed a divine right to rule. This essentially meant that their legitimacy was derived from divine approval and any act against them was also a sin against God.

The kings and queens who ruled Europe during this turbulent time laid the foundations of the modern world. Their actions ensured that the modern states we know would emerge, and many of our modern institutions date back to this era. The presumption of innocence in a legal case, the establishment of Protestantism or Catholicism as the dominant religion in various countries, and the limiting of royal power to the extent that the king was no longer above the law all stem from the choices made by kings and queens in the Middle Ages. Had they acted differently, our world might be entirely different.

Above: The Black Death did not strike everywhere at once. Its devastating effects could wreck an economy or make raising an army impossible for years to follow. Reports of plague had to be taken into account by commanders planning a campaign.

THE MIDDLE AGES WERE SHAPED BY A FEW EXTREMELY POWERFUL INDIVIDUALS. THE CHOICES THEY MADE HELPED TO SHAPE THE MODERN WORLD.

1

MILITARY LEADERS

No ruler of the Medieval period was solely a warrior: particularly in the Early Middle Ages, the ability to lead a force by example was critical to retaining power. Armies were prone to rout if their leader were killed or if he fled, and noblemen were sworn to stand with their king so long as he remained on the field. The personal leadership and fighting ability of a monarch were thus vital to victory in battle.

MARTIAL PROWESS was not just about direct combat. A ruler was wise to display his fighting abilities whenever possible and to remind both followers and potential foes of his capabilities. Success in tournaments or public displays of skill served to reinforce the confidence of those who were expected to follow their king into battle, and to intimidate those who might face him.

A reputation as a fierce and effective warmaker was useful in negotiations or as a deterrent to aggression. It was also a 'kingly' quality that enhanced the ruler's standing among his fellows as well as members of his own nobility. The effects were often

Opposite: The Battle of Hastings was a clash between the warriors of the 'Viking Age' and the armoured cavalry of the Middle Ages. Norman victory marked the beginning of a new era in European history.

subtle. It is not possible to say how many wisely negotiated treaties were made possible by a king's skill with a sword, even if it were never drawn in anger. Likewise, dynastic marriages had enormous long-term effects, but a good marriage required a demonstration of suitability that went beyond the wealth of a kingdom or the potential political benefits.

Thus the kings – and some of the queens – of the medieval era had to at the very least look the part of the effective warrior, and many were required to fight long and bitter campaigns for the survival of their realm. Wars are the most graphic instruments of change, and their winners shaped the course of history. The great warriors of Europe might not have personally written the history books, but their victories allowed them to dictate what was recorded and what would be forgotten.

CHARLEMAGNE (800–814)
Frankish Emperor and founder of the Carolingian Dynasty

After the fall of the Western Roman Empire, the Franks fared much better than many other groups, not least due to their prowess in warfare. It was a Frankish army, allied to Roman forces, that turned back the Hunnish invasion of Europe in 451 CE, and by the end of the century the Franks ruled most of the former Roman province of Gaul as well as parts of Germania. A unified kingdom was created by Clovis I (481–511), who also adopted the Orthodox Christian faith.

Named for Clovis' grandfather Merovech, the Merovingian dynasty ruled the Franks for nearly three centuries. Under the leadership of Charles Martel (686–741), the Franks turned back the Moorish invasion of Europe at the Battle of Tours (732). The later campaigns of Charles Martel integrated armoured cavalry into the Frankish mode of warfare, setting the stage for the rise of French chivalry.

Below: Charlemagne's position depended almost entirely upon his prowess as a war leader. Later rulers might derive their legitimacy from abstract concepts or continuance of an established line, but Charlemagne had to prove it in constant warfare.

The Merovingian dynasty weathered troubled times despite the kingdom being repeatedly divided and reunified, but eventually gave way to the Carolingian Dynasty founded by Charles the Great, better known as Charlemagne. Charlemagne's father was Pepin the Short (c. 714–768), son of Charles Martel. Pepin was a great war leader, winning the favour of the Pope and the distant Byzantine Empire, but his reign was plagued by endless revolts. Pepin's son Charles (later known as Charlemagne) became co-ruler of the Franks with his brother Carloman upon their father's death in 768, and sole ruler after Carloman's death in 771.

CHARLEMAGNE MADE EXTENSIVE USE OF ARMOURED CAVALRY, WHICH WOULD BECOME THE HALLMARK OF WARFARE IN THE MIDDLE AGES.

Like his father, Charles was favourably inclined towards the Pope and zealously spread Christianity throughout his realm. In 772, Pope Adrian I requested assistance against the Lombards of northern Italy, to which Charles responded with a campaign that made him master of the region. Although crowned king of the Lombards in 774, Charles had to put down revolts for some years to come. He campaigned into southern Italy in 787, gaining territory, but never completely conquering the region.

In the meantime, Charles fought savagely against the Saxons on several occasions. His motives were both political and religious; the Saxons worshipped pagan gods and Charles was an exponent of Christianity. Subjugated tribes were forced to accept baptism or be killed, leading to the massacre of 4500 Saxon leaders near Verden in 782. The executions by beheading were in part a punishment for rebellion and in part for Paganism, and had mixed results. The Saxons were subdued for a time, and other potential rebels might have been deterred, but it is equally possible that Verden was a rallying cry for future rebels.

Campaigns against the Saxons continued throughout Charles' reign, interspersed with other conquests. These often brought new problems, such as when the Avars, then dwelling in Hungary, attacked Bavaria, which Charles had recently added to his territory. Subdual of the Avars was interrupted by

Above: The Battle of Roncevaux Pass was a straightforward military disaster. It was later romanticized as a tale of tragic heroism, acquiring a status similar to that of the legends of King Arthur in Britain.

more Saxon revolts, but by 803 the Avars had been crushed and forced to accept Christianity.

Charlemagne's reign was characterized by near-constant warfare, and he was mostly successful. However, his most famous military campaign was a disaster. Envoys from Moorish realms in Spain requested help against the Emir of Cordoba. In return for their submission, Charles agreed to assist, perhaps seeing a chance to spread Christianity. However, his army was defeated before Saragossa, forcing the Franks into a retreat through the Pass of Roncesvalles.

During the retreat, the rearguard was attacked by the Basques, who Charles had thought pacified, and several high-ranking Frankish leaders were killed. The incident was immortalized in an epic poem written four centuries later. *The Song of Roland*, which tells of the heroic stand of Roland and the 12 Paladins, is not historically accurate, but forms part of the body of literature known as 'The Matter of France'. Rather than regional rulers loyal to Charles, the Paladins of the poem are perfect Christian knights; archetypes of a concept found throughout medieval and later literature. Later campaigns in Spain were more successful, with the Franks conquering a large expanse of territory by 812. The Balearic Islands had also fallen under Frankish control by 800.

With territory stretching from Spain to the Danube and the Baltic, Charles became known as Charles the Great, or

Charlemagne. His achievements were recognized by the Pope in 800, when he was crowned Emperor of the Romans on Christmas Day. Always having had a love of scholarship, Charlemagne sponsored centres of learning and implemented economic reforms. His sponsorship of a standardized script led to the Carolingian Minuscule becoming the standard for written Latin across Europe.

The widespread copying of older manuscripts into this new style resulted in the survival of a great many medieval texts that might otherwise have been lost. The style was revived during the Renaissance, and was influential in the development of more recent typefaces. Thus, although Charlemagne was first and foremost a warrior, his legacy was one of learning as well as furthering the Christianization of Europe.

WILLIAM THE CONQUEROR (1028–1087)
First Norman king of England

The so-called 'Viking Age' began in 793 with a small-scale raid on Lindisfarne. It ended in 1066, when the disputed succession to the throne of England was settled with the victory of William of Normandy over an Anglo-Saxon army commanded by Harold Godwinson. In the intervening years, the raids of the Norsemen grew ever grander in scale, until they were fielding thousands of men in hundreds of ships.

One solution to these large-scale raids was to bribe the Norsemen to go elsewhere – ideally into the territory of rivals – but King Charles III of West Francia, a descendant of Charlemagne, came up with a more lasting solution. Charles met with Rollo, leader of a large Viking force, and offered him territory along the northern coast of what is today France in return for fealty. Rollo agreed, becoming the first duke of what became known as Normandy. He ruled until 928 and was succeeded by his son, William Longsword.

The Norse settlers brought a fierce energy to their new lands and were an effective buffer against raids or invasions by their Scandinavian kinsmen. They integrated with the Frankish

Below: Rollo appears in medieval texts as a leader of the Norsemen who besieged Paris in 885–886. He may have been a Dane or a Norwegian; writers of the time used these terms more or less interchangeably.

population, gradually moving from an infantry-based, sea-mobile form of warfare to one making extensive use of armoured cavalry. These newly minted Normans were a potent military force, and were considered by many the finest fighting men in Europe. They served as mercenaries and undertook their own adventures, notably carving out a kingdom in Sicily.

By the early 1060s, Normandy was ruled by Duke William, who was no stranger to military adventurism. An illegitimate son of Duke Robert I (1000–1035), the young Duke William had to contend with the intrigues of Norman nobles seeking to use him as a figurehead for their own agendas, and was not secure in his position until around 1060.

Meanwhile, Edward the Confessor, King of England (1003–1066), had produced no heirs, creating a disputed succession. William of Normandy was related to Edward by way of his mother, Emma of Normandy, who was granddaughter to William Longsword. William thus had a claim to the throne of England, but so did Harald Hardrada (1015–1066), King of Norway. The preferred candidate among the English was Harold Godwinson, Earl of Wessex.

THE NORMANS EMPLOYED AN EARLY VERSION OF TACTICS LATER USED VERY SUCCESSFULLY BY THE ENGLISH. THEIR ARMOURED CAVALRY DELIVERED POWERFUL BLOWS TO AN ENEMY WEAKENED BY HARASSING ARCHERS.

There is considerable controversy over the legitimacy of any of these claims, with accusations that Harold Godwinson had sworn to support William's claim to the throne of England. It was also alleged that the throne had been offered to William by emissaries and that Edward the Confessor had indicated that he wanted Harold to succeed him. The truth will likely never be known, but in any case the witanagemot, an assembly of English nobility, selected Harold and crowned him king.

The first challenge to Harold's rule came from Harald Hardrada, who was defeated at Stamford Bridge. This was a clash between similar forces; both the Norsemen and the Anglo-Saxons favoured combat on foot. Afterwards, Harold marched quickly south to meet William's army, which had crossed the Channel and established itself in the southeast of England.

The Norman style of combat was very different to that of their opponents. The primary striking arm was the cavalry, armed with long spears and swords and protected by chainmail armour. Backed up by archers and infantry, the Norman force had the advantage of being able to use combined-arms tactics, showering the English with arrows between cavalry charges. After a hard fight, with the issue in real doubt at times, the English were defeated and Harold killed.

This did not yield William instant control of the country. The Anglo-Saxons elected another king and tried to resist as William secured his line of communications and built temporary fortifications to protect his territories in the southeast. After returning to Normandy for a while, William resumed his campaigning in England in 1067, and again in 1068. In addition

Above: After his victory at Hastings, William still faced opposition. It was not until the end of 1066 that he captured London and received the surrender of the newly-appointed king of the English, Edgar the Aetheling.

HARALD HARDRADA

HARALD, better known by the nickname Hardrada ('Stern Counsel' or perhaps 'Stern Ruler'), was the son of a Norwegian chieftain, and may or may not have had a blood claim to the crown of Norway. His family were involved in the power struggles then besetting Norway, and Harald's first military experience was of defeat. He left Norway for Kievan Rus, eventually becoming a commander of the Varangian Guard in Byzantium. There he had many adventures, but ultimately had to return home to avoid being imprisoned or put to death.

Now a wealthy and experienced leader, Harald made a challenge for the crown of Norway, which resulted in a compromise whereby he would rule Norway under the authority of the king of Denmark. His attempt to claim kingship of the whole realm led to years of inconclusive warfare, after which Harald made a play for England instead.

Harald made an alliance with Tostig Godwinson, brother of Harold Godwinson, who had been chosen as king of England, and invaded at the head of an army that included adventurers from many Norse lands. Initially successful at the Battle of Fulford, he was ultimately defeated at Stamford Bridge by Harold Godwinson, who was in turn killed by William the Conqueror at Hastings. Harald Hardrada's attempt to gain the crown of England was the culmination of a lifetime of adventure and risk, earning him the epithet 'The Last Viking'.

to opposition from the Anglo-Saxons, he also faced attacks from Denmark and revolts in previously conquered lands.

To secure his power, William had castles built all over the country. Initially simple constructions of earth and wood, these fortifications were later rebuilt in stone as a powerful symbol of Norman rule. Great churches and cathedrals were also built, serving to remind all that viewed them of the power and prestige of the Normans.

Gradually, the Norman style of feudal rule replaced the earlier Anglo-Saxon system. As his ancestor Duke Richard I of Normandy had fostered the growth of feudalism in Normandy, now William brought it to England. In so doing, he set the pattern for generations to come, and established a system of nobility that still exists – albeit in a hugely evolved form – in England today.

PHILIP II (PHILIP AUGUSTUS) (1165–1223)

Gained territory at the expense of the Angevin Empire

At the time the future Philip II of France was born, nations in the modern sense did not exist. A monarch's realm was defined by a chain of allegiances from the owner of a territory to his monarch, regardless of where that territory lay. Those chains could become entangled, often as a result of dynastic marriages. Thus, most of what was geographically France was the property of the English crown in 1165.

King Henry II of England (1133–1189) was also Count of Anjou and Duke of Normandy, and acquired Aquitaine by marriage in 1152. He was of the house of Angevin, and his enormous territory became known as the Angevin Empire. This situation was not to the liking of the French nobility, and caused additional friction in an already difficult relationship. Among the issues was one of homage. As a senior French nobleman, the king of England was expected to pay homage to the king of France. Demands to do so and the conflict arising from refusal – or the weakening of position that accompanied acquiescence – were part of the complex political games played throughout that period of history.

Philip II was crowned king of France in 1179, though his father did not die until the following year. He reached an understanding with Henry II of England, freeing himself from the control of his own powerful nobility. This was not without incident: in 1185

Below: In the Middle Ages territories were defined by feudal relationships rather than formal borders in the modern sense. Philip II took the throne at a time when much of France owed allegiance to the king of England.

FRANCE AT THE ACCESSION OF PHILIP AUGUSTUS

Boundary of French Kingdom thus
Domains of the French Crown
Subject to Henry II
Claimed by Henry II

Philip had to put down a revolt, but emerged as the sole ruler of a reasonably well unified France. This enabled Philip to undertake a campaign against the English holdings in France, beginning in 1187. Clever negotiations following military victories created gains for Philip without triggering a large-scale conflict.

In 1189, Henry II of England died and was succeeded by his son Richard I ('The Lionheart'), who spent only a few months in England during his entire reign. The rest of the time he was at home in Aquitaine, on campaign, or held in captivity. Chief among his campaigns was the Third Crusade (1189–1192), in which Philip II also participated. Philip and Richard were uneasy allies during the crusade, and when Philip became ill he decided to return to France. There, he took advantage of Richard I's absence to conquer more English territory in France.

Richard I attempted to return home to deal with the problem, but was captured near Vienna by Leopold V, Duke of Austria, and imprisoned by the Holy Roman Emperor until a ransom could be paid. Philip II of France was one of those who offered additional payments to the emperor – but in this case it was to hold Richard prisoner for a while longer.

PHILIP II WAS A STATESMAN AS WELL AS A WARRIOR. HIS MILITARY VICTORIES WERE TRANSLATED INTO LASTING ADVANTAGE BY SHREWD PEACE NEGOTIATIONS.

In the interim, Philip II made additional gains against Angevin territories in France, and continued to do so even after Richard I was released to take command of his armies. The conflict was characterized by periods of fighting followed by a truce and negotiations, with Philip suffering defeats as well as winning victories. His situation was improved by the death of Richard I in 1199 as a result of a wound inflicted by a crossbowman.

Richard I left no legitimate heirs, and named his brother John as successor. This caused divisions within the Angevin Empire, as some nobles preferred other candidates, but in 1200 Philip II agreed to recognize John's titles over the Angevin lands in France in return for some territories. This arrangement lasted until 1202, when war broke out again.

King John abandoned the war in France to his subordinates and went back to England, allowing Philip to conquer Normandy.

Among his gains was the powerful and very advanced castle of Château Gaillard, which was besieged in 1203–04. Château Gaillard was one of King Richard's most notable achievements; its loss further reduced faith in his successor.

Further conflict resulted in more gains for Philip, but in 1214 he faced a coalition of English forces under King John and a vast array of European nobility led by the Holy Roman Emperor. Some were rebels against Philip's rule, some inspired by the Pope's disapproval, and some assisting their allies. Theirs was a powerful force, but disunited, a weakness Philip was able to exploit.

Marching his army to meet the allied force, Philip halted at Bouvines, where the terrain was favourable to him. He then simply waited until the allies played into his hands. The allied army was marching in the usual three

Above: Philip II almost met an untimely end when he was unhorsed at the Battle of Bouvines. A downed knight could be stabbed through gaps in his armour or simply bludgeoned to death.

'battles', and as the allied vanguard arrived its commanders did exactly what Philip had hoped; they launched an immediate charge without waiting for support. The remainder of the allied force joined in as it arrived, attacking piecemeal against Philip's prepared forces. Even so, the French were hard pressed and their king unhorsed, but with the initial shock blunted, the outnumbered French were able to grind down their enemies and eventually rout them.

Victory at Bouvines left Philip II virtually unchallenged throughout the rest of his reign. He died in 1223, leaving behind a vastly more powerful France than he had inherited, and a greatly diminished English presence in France. In so doing he made possible the ascendance of France and the eventual loss of all English territory there.

ALEXANDER NEVSKY (1221–1263)

Defender of Russia against German and Swedish invaders

There is some doubt as to exactly who the people known as the Rus were, but it seems likely that theirs was a fusion of Slavic and Scandinavian cultures. If this hypothesis is correct, population pressure and their natural tendency to seek out new

THE ANGEVIN EMPIRE

THE NOBILITY OF EUROPE included three great noble houses referred to as Angevin, meaning 'of Anjou'. Among them was the Plantagenet dynasty of England, founded by Henry II. In addition to the holdings of the English crown, Henry inherited Normandy and Anjou. His marriage to Eleanor of Aquitaine brought her extensive territories under Henry's control as well.

This created the potentially difficult situation where the king of England was also a vassal of the king of France – although only in his capacity as a landholder in France. The French kings of the era, for their part, wanted to return the lands of the Angevin Empire to French control. Philip II proceeded slowly and carefully in this regard, gaining small areas by negotiation after a limited conflict.

Later conflict over former English holdings in France, and what little remained to the English crown after the reign of King John I, would lead to the Hundred Years' War. This was a rather different conflict to that waged by Philip II. Philip's wars were territorial readjustments between feudal landholders, whereas the later conflict was between the states of England and France and had some of the character of modern inter-state conflicts.

Left: Eleanor of Aquitaine is buried at Fontevraud Abbey. Her marriage to Henry II of England was of profound importance to that realm, not only in terms of territory gained, but also her governance whilst Richard I was absent.

opportunities caused the Scandinavian people to push eastwards, entering the lands of Slavic tribes some time before the ninth century. These warlike new arrivals soon became a warrior elite within the society of their homelands, rising to the upper echelons in return for leadership and protection.

Initially centred on Novgorod and later Kiev, the Rus expanded their territory and absorbed more Slavic tribes, developing a culture of their own that formed the basis of more modern Russian society. Reaching its peak in the early eleventh century, Kievan Rus was in decline when the Mongols arrived on its eastern fringes.

The Mongol Empire was an alliance of tribal confederations united under Temujin Borjigin (1162–1227), better known as Genghis Khan. Where previously the tribes had been capable only of making themselves a nuisance, united they were able to carve out the largest empire the world has ever seen, and to do so in a remarkably short time. The title of Genghis Khan was bestowed upon Temujin in 1206, at which point the Mongol Empire came into being. By 1223, the Mongols had come into conflict with the Kievan Rus, whose forces were defeated even though they outnumbered the Mongols by a large margin.

Above: Alexander Nevsky took holy orders before his death and was popularly considered a saint thereafter. He was canonized in 1547, and much later his remains were moved to St Petersburg on the orders of Peter the Great.

It was at this fraught point in Russian history that Alexander Yaroslavich was born. Second son of the prince of Vladimir, one of medieval Russia's capitals, he was requested by the city of Novgorod to become their Knyaz. This title can be variously translated as 'prince' or 'duke', and in this case denoted a nobleman designated as the city's war-leader, but with little peacetime political power.

Novgorod was under threat from Swedish forces, for complex reasons including conflict with Finnish tribes and an ongoing dispute over trade routes passing through its territory. In 1240, hearing that a Scandinavian fleet had landed and troops were marching towards Lake Ladoga, Prince Alexander Yaroslavich came out with his force to meet them. Accounts of the battle

ALEXANDER NEVSKY IS WIDELY
CONSIDERED THE GREATEST OF
RUSSIAN HEROES. HIS NAME IS
TRADITIONALLY ASSOCIATED WITH
RUSSIAN WARSHIPS.

vary, but it seems that Prince Alexander
caught the Swedes by surprise and routed
them at the River Neva. For this feat he
gained the title 'Nevsky'.

Alexander Nevsky rapidly fell out of
favour in Novgorod, probably as a result of
meddling in political affairs that were beyond
his remit. He was dismissed, but reinstated
two years later when Novgorod was again threatened from
the west. This time it was the Teutonic Knights, on a crusade
to Christianize the largely pagan lands of the Rus, assisted by
Swedes, Danes, Norwegians and Finns with their own agenda,
but sharing an enmity towards Novgorod.

The Crusader force was not well organized, marching in three separate groups too widely separated to assist one another. This permitted the Rus to defeat them in detail, beginning with the Swedes who were again defeated on the banks of the River Neva. The Danish force did better, getting close to Novgorod and capturing the town of Kaporye.

Meanwhile, the Teutonic Knights began advancing towards Lake Peipus with their supporting forces, routing a rather ill-advised counterattack by local militia and capturing Pskov. Alexander Nevsky first retook Kaporye, then launched a raid that drew the Crusaders out of Pskov. Despite being heavily outnumbered, the Crusaders were heartened by victory in a skirmish and followed Nevsky's force onto the frozen surface of

Below: The 'battle on the ice' at Lake Peipus has been the subject of art, film and music. Its legendary status has perhaps come at the cost of historical inaccuracy, with dramatized events from the 1938 film recalled as fact in some cases.

THE MONGOL EMPIRE

IN THE EARLY TWELFTH century, the people of the Mongolian steppe and surrounding areas were divided into a great many tribes, who negated much of their potential power by warring among themselves. The Mongol tribe arose to prominence among them and achieved military success against the Jin Empire of northern China, but soon fragmented. As a result, when Temujin was born in 1167, his tribe was small and powerless, a situation made much worse when his father was killed while Temujin was still a boy.

Despite these difficult beginnings, Temujin managed to put together an alliance that subjugated other Mongol tribes, and in 1204 he took the title Chingis Khan (Great Khan), normally rendered in the West as Genghis Khan. Despite being a confederation of tribes, his Mongol Empire was highly organized, with a clear chain of command and the capability of carrying out complex orders. This permitted the conquest of northern China, although it was necessary to force Chinese engineers to assist with the subjugation of fortified cities.

The Mongols then moved west, overrunning the Khwarazmian Empire of Persia. The Mongols' superior mobility made the Khwarazmian strategy of relying on fortifications and local garrisons ineffective, and most of the empire was subjugated in Genghis' lifetime. Upon his death in 1227, his empire was divided among his sons, with Ogodei as senior. In this division lay the beginnings of the empire's fragmentation into khanates, but it remained powerful for the time being.

The Mongol Empire subjugated the Kievan Rus and defeated attempts to halt its advance into Poland and Hungary. The death of Ogodei in 1242 caused the Mongols to turn back, and soon afterwards the empire fragmented, with the western portion becoming known as the Golden Horde. The Mongol Empire remained a potent force, but its nature gradually changed. The fifth and last great khan, Kublai Khan, technically held the allegiance of all the Mongol clans, but in practice concerted action was problematic. Kublai Khan himself was less of a nomad warlord and more of a Chinese emperor.

After Kublai Khan's death in 1294, the khanates went their own way, although the Golden Horde remained a powerful factor in the politics of eastern Europe until the death of Timur Lenk in 1405. Even then, the fragmented khanates continued to command tribute from nearby states until finally driven out by expanding Russian power in 1502.

Lake Peipus. Despite the departure of some of their supporting troops, disheartened by the size of Nevsky's army, the Crusaders launched a headlong attack that was blunted by archery and well-chosen defensive terrain. Nevsky's cavalry then fell on the Crusader flanks, grinding their force down by superior numbers.

The battle on the ice has been depicted in film, with the Russians breaking the ice to destroy their foes. This is unlikely to have happened in reality. Instead, Nevsky's excellent tactics, such as concentrating his archers where they could shoot into the enemy's unshielded flank, won the day. Defeat at Lake Peipus forced the Teutonic Order to withdraw from the region.

Alexander Nevsky made a wise choice when faced with the Mongol threat. Rather than a hopeless resistance, he chose to side with them and became their regional governor. When his brother Andrey rebelled against Mongol rule, Alexander defeated him and was appointed Grand Prince of Russia by the Mongol overlords. This was the origin of the Russian Tsars, and Nevsky was canonized as a saint in 1547.

Opposite: The Mongol Empire created by Genghis Khan was an artefact of his personality. Divisions emerged almost immediately after Genghis' death, though the empire did not fragment into khanates until the death of Kublai, its fifth Great Khan.

WLADYSLAW II JAGIELLO (1386–1434)
Defender of Poland-Lithuania against the Teutonic Knights

The Hunnish invasion of Europe left some regions sparsely populated, notably what is today Poland, and from the fifth century onwards Slavic people began to migrate into these areas. Despite incursions by Huns, Avars and other nomadic people, they prospered and built towns that gradually became centres of power. By the late tenth century, a unified state had come to exist, but it fragmented soon afterwards.

By the time of Wladyslaw I (1260–1333), Poland was divided into many small states. Wladyslaw I was elected prince of Great Poland in 1296, but was later deposed in favour of Wenceslas II of Bavaria (1271–1305). With the approval of the Pope and assistance from Hungary, Wladyslaw I was able to conquer Little Poland and later Great Poland. He extended his holdings

Below: Wladyslaw I, father of Casimir The Great, died as king of a unified Poland. His life was characterized by political and military struggles, paving the way for eventual union with Lithuania, which created the largest Christian state in Europe.

into Pomerania, but lost them in 1308 to the Teutonic Knights. Despite this, Wladyslaw I was crowned king of a reunified Poland in 1320.

Wladyslaw I died in 1333 and was succeeded by his son Casimir, whose reign was sufficiently successful that he became known as 'The Great'. In 1325, Casimir was married to Aldona-Ona, daughter of the duke of Lithuania. Although the marriage produced no heirs, it represented a reconciliation between Poland and its former enemy Lithuania, and in 1386 Jogaila, grand duke of Lithuania, married Queen Jadwiga of Poland, co-ruling until her death in 1399, after which he was sole king of Poland.

Known as Wladyslaw II Jagiello after his baptism and marriage, Jogaila founded the Jagiellonian dynasty that ruled both Poland and Lithuania until 1572. The unified Poland-Lithuania was one of the most powerful European states at the time, but faced challenges from the Teutonic Order, who were intent on Christianizing Lithuania. Although Jogaila had converted Lithuania to Christianity in 1387, the Teutonic Knights remained unconvinced of his sincerity – or they may have used this as a pretext for political reasons.

In 1409, Lithuanian support for an uprising in Teutonic territory led to the outbreak of hostilities. The Teutonic Knights represented a powerful concentration of military capability in a relatively small force, and were aware that their best chance lay in offensive action. They launched an invasion of Poland and were initially very successful against the unprepared Polish forces. A truce followed, in which political gambits were attempted with the intent of dividing Poland and Lithuania.

These measures failed, and a joint Polish-Lithuanian army marched on the Teutonic Knights' stronghold at Marienberg. This caught the knights out of position, not least due to Jogaila's strategy of using diversionary raids to

Below: After his marriage to Queen Jadwiga of Poland, Duke Jogaila of Lithuania took the name Wladyslaw, ruling as Wladislaw II Jagiello. The two founded a dynasty that ruled Poland for most of the next two centuries.

disguise his line of march. The knights had expected Polish and Lithuanian forces to march separately, and to be able to defeat each in turn by aggressive attacks launched from a central position. In the event, they were forced to meet the whole invading force under a united command.

Both forces contained contingents from neighbouring states, allies and other groups including mercenaries and crusaders intent on assisting their brethren. Among the Polish-Lithuanian force were Mongol cavalry, while the Teutonic Knights were equipped with primitive cannon. These played little part in the battle, however.

The Teutonic plan was to provoke their enemies into attacking a defensive position, then unleash their armoured cavalry in a powerful counterattack. To this end they sent a gift of two swords to Jogaila, with the implication that he needed help from his enemies. The gambit did not work particularly well, although after the initial clash the Lithuanian contingent began to retreat. This

Above: The Battle of Tannenberg was a microcosm of European politics at the time. The fighting involved contingents from all over Europe and even a force of Mongols, whilst primitive cannon were employed to little effect.

Opposite: Edward I of England was instrumental in putting John Balliol on the Scottish throne, but invaded and deposed him after the Scots made alliance with France. Edward took the Stone of Scone to England with him when he left Scotland.

has been represented as a deliberate feigned retreat to draw the enemy from their positions, but such claims are always suspect.

The timely commitment of the Polish-Lithuanian reserve stabilized the situation, enabling the Lithuanians to rally and return to the fighting. In the end, the Teutonic force was driven back to its fortified camp and made a stand there before being soundly defeated. Accounts of the battle vary in numbers, events and even name, with Polish accounts typically referring to the battle as Grunwald and German writers naming it for the nearby village of Tannenberg.

Several Teutonic fortresses were captured in the wake of the battle, but a siege of their capital at Marienberg was unsuccessful. Renewed Teutonic offensives were defeated at Koronowo later in the year, and the Order never recovered from its losses. Despite further clashes, Jogaila was able to bring the Teutonic threat to Poland to an end, and the Battle of Grunwald/ Tannenberg passed into the mythology of several nations – often with very different versions of events.

ROBERT THE BRUCE (1274–1329)

Champion of Scottish independence and victor at Bannockburn

Robert the Bruce's early life was lived against the backdrop of a dynastic crisis in Scotland. King Alexander III was killed in an accident in 1286, having outlived both his sons. Alexander had, in 1284, made provision for his young granddaughter Margaret to inherit, but her death in 1290 left no clear line of succession. Scotland at that time had no legislation for such a situation, and the resulting dispute was exploited by Edward I of England.

LACK OF CLEAR RULES GOVERNING SUCCESSION WITHOUT AN OBVIOUS HEIR EVENTUALLY LED TO ROBERT THE BRUCE BECOMING KING OF SCOTLAND.

Eventually, John Balliol of Galway was chosen as king, a solution favourable to Edward and to many Scots – at least at first. John Balliol was crowned in 1292, but Edward I soon began treating Scotland as a puppet kingdom and undermining Balliol's rule. The result, inevitably, was conflict between England and Scotland. After a series of raids, an English army invaded

Above: Stirling Castle was a pivotal location in the struggles between England and Scotland, with control of the castle essential to military operations deeper into enemy territory. It was thus the site of repeated clashes.

Scotland and forced John Balliol to surrender. He went into exile after abdicating in 1296, leaving Scotland again without a king.

One of the other contenders for the throne had been Robert Bruce, grandfather of Robert the Bruce. The family had rebelled against the installation of the infant Margaret, and harboured resentment that would fuel their involvement in the wars to come. The Bruces declined to recognize John Balliol and later chose to support the rebellion led by William Wallace against the English, instead of putting it down as they had been ordered to do.

Wallace won a notable victory in 1297 against an invading English army at the battle of Stirling Bridge, but was defeated at Falkirk in 1298. Wallace was eclipsed and eventually betrayed to the English in 1305. Leadership of the Scots fell jointly upon Robert the Bruce and John the Red Comyn, who were enemies.

THE BATTLE OF STIRLING BRIDGE (1297)

IN THE LATE THIRTEENTH century, conventional wisdom held that a body of infantry could be routed by the charge of armoured cavalry, and even those that stood their ground would fall prey to the superior fighting power of the mounted knight. The Scottish rebellion against the rule of Edward I of England led by William Wallace consisted largely of valiant but under-equipped footsoldiers, who were not expected to be able to resist the English charge.

Wallace had succeeded in liberating many castles and fortified towns from the English, notably Stirling Castle, which commanded a crossing of the River Forth and was considered a gateway to Scotland.

He camped his force on the north side of the Forth and awaited the approach of the English, who initially sent footsoldiers across Stirling Bridge, but then pulled them back.

The English cavalry then advanced. Wallace waited until a significant but manageable number had crossed the narrow bridge then attacked, sending men to chop down the bridge supports. The advance force was cut off and massacred, causing the remainder of the English army to retreat in disarray. This was a rare instance of footsoldiers attacking cavalry, and on this occasion the gambit worked spectacularly well due to Wallace's careful choice of location.

Left: The destruction of Stirling Bridge to cut off a manageable portion of the English army was a masterstroke on the part of William Wallace, but one that could not be repeated on other occasions.

Below: Robert the Bruce was defeated by Edward I of England, but proved more than a match for his son Edward II. His victory at Bannockburn is still a source of Scottish national pride.

In 1302, Robert the Bruce surrendered to the English rather than fight alongside John, and in 1306 stabbed his rival in a dispute that – ironically – may have started as an earnest attempt to win his rival's support.

Robert the Bruce was chosen by the Scots to be their new king, which was not to the liking of Edward I. Robert was deposed by an English army and forced to flee to Ireland, but eventually returned to fight a guerrilla campaign against the English. His opponent was Edward II, who had succeeded to the throne upon the death of his father and who was not such a great warrior.

The decisive clash between England and Scotland came in 1314, by which time Robert the Bruce had recaptured most of the castles held by the English in Scotland. He laid siege to Stirling Castle, an important gateway between England and Scotland as it controlled crossings of the River Forth; as was the custom of the time, the garrison commander had agreed to surrender if not relieved by midsummer.

Edward II marched to the relief of his castle, confident in the abilities of his army, which combined the strengths of armoured cavalry and archers. On the Scots side, there were far less cavalry; most of their strength were free men armed with pikes, lightly armoured if at all, but effective against unsupported cavalry.

An initial attempt to force passage through to the castle was turned back by determined pikemen, after which nightfall precluded further combat. During the night, Edward II made a serious tactical error by trying to redeploy before dawn. First light found his men-at-arms mired in marshy ground and greatly disordered, a situation enthusiastically exploited by the Scots pikemen.

King Edward barely escaped the disaster, first trying to enter Stirling Castle. He was turned away, since the garrison were bound by oath to surrender if not relieved and would have had to give him up as a prisoner. He managed to escape to Dunbar and thence to England, ruling until deposed in 1327.

In the meantime, Robert the Bruce was declared rightful king of Scotland by the Declaration of Arbroath in 1320, and in 1324 his sovereignty was recognized by the Pope. An earlier agreement between France and Scotland was also renewed, promising mutual support against England in the event that either was attacked.

During his subsequent reign, Robert the Bruce tried to create an alliance between Ireland and Scotland against England, campaigning in Ireland in support of his brother Edward, who was crowned High King of Ireland in 1316. The death of Edward Bruce in battle brought this ambition to an end.

Robert was finally recognized by the English crown as king of Scotland in 1328, but died a year later. His only unfulfilled ambition was to go on crusade, and he arranged for his heart to be carried by a force of crusading Scottish knights. This expedition never reached the Holy Land, however, and Robert the Bruce's heart was returned to Scotland to be buried at Melrose Abbey.

Above: Despite modern claims of a force of Knights Templar on the Scottish side and other novelties, the reality of Scottish victory at Bannockburn is simple: the English put themselves in a bad position and the Scots took full advantage.

EDWARD III OF ENGLAND (1312–1377)

Architect of English military supremacy

After his ignominious defeat at Bannockburn in 1314, the position of Edward II, king of England, was extremely weak, and only divisions among his enemies saved him from disaster. The situation improved after 1318 with the support and guidance of Hugh de Despenser, but Edward's rampant favouritism gradually alienated his supporters. Among those who turned against him was his wife, Isabella of France.

In 1325, Isabella went to France with her son, Edward of Windsor (the future Edward III), who was to take up his position as Duke of Aquitaine and pay homage to the French king in that capacity. There, she formed an alliance with the exiled Roger Mortimer and in 1326 they returned to England to depose Edward II and his favourites. Edward II was forced to abdicate in favour of his son, and was imprisoned in the hope he would quietly die. When he did not do so, he was eventually put to death.

The young king Edward III was initially merely a figurehead for Isabella and Mortimer, but grew in power until in 1330 he imprisoned Mortimer and soon afterwards had him executed. Edward's mother retired from public life thereafter, and Edward III began trying to rebuild the fortunes of his realm. The defeat at Bannockburn and the subsequent ravaging of northern England would be avenged by deposing the Scottish king and restoring English control.

King Robert of Scotland, victor of Bannockburn, and his most able supporters had all recently died, leaving the young David II on the throne without strong support. Taking advantage of this, Edward Balliol (son of John Balliol, who had earlier contended the Scottish throne) and a group of exiled Scottish noblemen made a bid for the throne with English support. Edward Balliol was crowned king of Scotland in 1332, but was chased out of the country mere months later.

Edward III launched a campaign against the Scots, winning

EDWARD II SOWED THE SEEDS OF HIS OWN DESTRUCTION AND WAS ULTIMATELY DEPOSED IN FAVOUR OF HIS SON, EDWARD III.

Opposite: The Battle of Halidon Hill demonstrated the effectiveness of combined-arms tactics against an enemy that had only one mode of attack. The Scottish attack was blunted by archery then driven back in hand-to-hand combat.

Above: This depiction of the Battle of Crécy is illustrative rather than factual. It is notable that archers are in the foreground, not knights.

a notable victory at Halidon Hill in 1333. Although modest in scope, the battle established the war-winning pattern used in many subsequent conflicts. Massed archers were drawn up on defensive terrain, protected by the armoured men-at-arms. As the enemy laboured towards them, the archers broke up their charge, with those who reached the English line dealt with by men-at-arms. At Halidon Hill it was massed Scots pikemen who were defeated, but the tactic would prove equally effective against the noble cavalry of France.

Edward Balliol was twice more installed as king of Scotland, but deposed each time, and as an ally of France David II made war upon England. This resulted in defeat at Neville's Cross in 1346, with David becoming a prisoner for 11 years. He was eventually ransomed, with a long truce agreed between England and Scotland.

Meanwhile, England was at war with France. The reasons were complex, but among them was the claim of Edward III to the throne of France. His rather ramshackle fleet comprehensively defeated a French force off Sluys in 1340 in what was essentially a land battle fought at sea, decided by boarding actions and archery support. This was the first major English victory of what would become known as the Hundred Years' War, and ended the possibility of a French invasion of England.

Landing at Cherbourg in 1346, Edward III launched a campaign that was essentially a large-scale raid to plunder the countryside and inflict economic damage. After getting nearly as far as Paris, but worn down by dysentery, the English host began retiring east. Edward's army made a forced crossing of the River Somme, supported by longbowmen, and drove off a force of crossbowmen sent to delay them long enough for the French army to catch up. As the English force continued its march towards safety, the French army made an attack on the rear of the column, and it was obvious that Edward had to deploy for battle or be overwhelmed.

Edward's chosen position was at Crécy-en-Ponthieu, where the terrain would funnel the French assault onto his archers. The following day, the French host made repeated charges uphill towards the waiting English, who repeated the tactics of Halidon Hill. Sloping ground and intense archery blunted the charges of the French heavy

VICTORY AT NEVILLE'S CROSS IN 1346 RESULTED IN A TRUCE WITH SCOTLAND, ENABLING EDWARD III TO TURN HIS FULL ATTENTION TO WAR WITH FRANCE.

Below: Edward III understood the importance of sea power. By gaining control over the English Channel he protected his own home territory and ensured he could land his army in France at a time of his choosing.

cavalry, enabling the English men-at-arms to repel those who reached the line. A few cannon also saw action but achieved little other than making a lot of noise.

Accounts of the Battle at Crécy suggest the French made at least fifteen charges at the English line, not counting local attacks by small groups. Amid the desperate combat, Edward III's son – also called Edward, but better known as the Black Prince – 'won his spurs' as a leader of fighting men. The French attacks were finally halted around midnight, and the English moved away under cover of darkness.

> ALONG WITH POITIERS AND AGINCOURT, CRÉCY WAS ONE OF THE THREE GREAT ENGLISH VICTORIES OF THE HUNDRED YEARS WAR.

Despite the heavy casualties inflicted upon the flower of French chivalry, the English did not so much win in the usual sense at Crécy as avoided defeat. Strategically, however, Edward III had gained a critical victory in that he had crippled French military power and extricated his imperilled army from a very bad situation. He also established the pattern for much of the Hundred Years' War. The combined-arms tactics of the English, complementing archery with the striking power of mounted men-at-arms or their defensive capabilities on foot, was established as a winning combination.

Edward III was successful in his later career, but was eclipsed by his sons, notably Edward the Black Prince and John of Gaunt. He left behind an effective military system well suited to war against France, medieval England's most constant of foes.

HENRY IV OF ENGLAND (1367–1413)
Fighting for a troubled crown

The title of duke was introduced to English nobility by Edward III, and was reserved for those closely related to the monarch. Duchies were given as appanages to sons of the monarch who would not inherit the kingdom, ensuring that they retained the wealth and power associated with a close royal relative without diluting the king's own power and status. Among them was John of Gaunt, First Duke of Lancaster and father of Henry Bolingbroke, Earl of Derby – who would one day be King Henry IV.

Opposite: Richard II of England came to the throne as a child, and was for several years a figurehead for his regents. Even after securing power in his own right, his position was sufficiently weak that he could be deposed by Henry Bolingbroke.

When Richard, son of Edward the Black Prince and grandson of Edward III, was named his successor in 1377, powerful nobles sought to control the young king. The most prominent were referred to as the Lords Appellant, and among their gambits to retain control of the throne was the Merciless Parliament of 1388. Several of the king's favourites were accused of treason. Some escaped into exile, while others were put to death. Among these Lords Appellant were Thomas, Duke of Gloucester, and Henry, Earl of Derby.

Eventually, Richard II asserted his kingship as an adult and broke the power of the Lords Appellant. Some were treated quite leniently; others exiled or killed. Henry, Earl of Derby, was one of those who remained at court and apparently became a supporter of the king. However, in 1398, a year after being elevated to the rank of Duke of Hereford, he was banished as a result of a dispute with the Duke of Norfolk.

HENRY BOLINGBROKE WAS TO HAVE MET THE DUKE OF NORFOLK IN COMBAT TO RESOLVE THEIR DISPUTE, BUT BOTH WERE INSTEAD EXILED BY RICHARD II.

Richard II seems to have become complacent at this point; in 1399 he visited Ireland along with all of his close supporters, creating an opportunity for Henry to return from the continent. He encountered very slight opposition and was able to establish himself in a powerful position. Richard surrendered and was forced to abdicate, eventually dying during his imprisonment.

Henry IV's reign began with a rebellion by Richard's supporters in 1400 and troubles with both Scotland and France. No sooner was the situation stabilized than Owen Glendower led a revolt in Wales. Glendower had not been called to participate in the 1400 expedition to Scotland and was then accused of treason for failing to present himself, pushing him into revolt. Henry launched three unsuccessful campaigns into Wales, but the rebellion continued unabated. Indeed, Owen Glendower found new allies in the Percy family of Northumberland.

The Percys had captured the Scottish Earl of Douglas at the Battle of Homildon Hill in 1402, and were deeply offended when

Opposite: Owain Glyndwr (Owen Glendower) fought for England against the Scots before leading an initially very successful rebellion in Wales. He was never captured, and according to legend will return when Wales is again threatened.

Right: Henry Hotspur entertained hopes of assistance from Owen Glendower, but met the king's army unaided. Despite slaying several of Henry IV's decoys, Hotspur's force fled the field when he was killed.

King Henry IV demanded Douglas be handed over to him. They had been hoping for a huge ransom and would not now receive it. Instead, when King Henry refused their demand that he instead ransom Edmund Mortimer from captivity in Wales, they freed Douglas in return for his agreement to fight alongside them and rose in rebellion against the king. The decisive clash came at Shrewsbury in 1403 and is famous for the defeat of Henry Percy, who was known as Hotspur for his warlike and energetic nature.

Henry was warned that several notable warriors had sworn to kill him in the coming battle, and arranged for knights to act as decoys while he fought in plain armour. Sure enough, the doubles were all killed – the Earl of Douglas proclaimed that he had slain three kings that day, but more kept appearing – while Henry acquitted himself well in anonymity. The Battle of Shrewsbury resulted in temporary pacification of the north and further rebellion was also put down, leading to Henry ordering

Opposite: Henry IV faced opposition throughout his troubled reign. His chief opponents were Owen Glendower and the powerful Percy family led by Henry Percy, Earl of Northumberland and father of Henry 'Hotspur'.

the execution of the Archbishop of York as one of the instigators. Henry's subsequent ill health was blamed upon divine displeasure over this act.

Benefiting from French assistance, Owen Glendower meanwhile came to control most of Wales by 1405. However, Henry IV's son (the future Henry V) began to make gains against them and by 1409 the rebellion was essentially over. Owen Glendower's wife and children were captured and his own fate remains unclear.

HENRY V EARNED DISTINCTION AS A WAR LEADER IN THE SERVICE OF HIS FATHER, NOTABLY IN OPPOSING OWEN GLENDOWER'S WELSH REBELLION.

Henry's ill health led to the realm being governed for a time by an appointed council, and his later years were eclipsed by the deeds of his sons. He died in 1413, having established a stable succession for his son Henry V despite the weakness of his own claim to the throne and vigorous opposition from his enemies.

HENRY V OF ENGLAND (1387–1422)

Victor of Agincourt and master of the English Channel

The future Henry V was the son of Henry Bolingbroke, then Earl of Derby. Upon his father's exile in 1398 he remained at court and apparently enjoyed a cordial relationship with King Richard II. When Henry Bolingbroke returned and became king of England, Henry was the heir apparent and campaigned on behalf of his father.

The future Henry V fought against the Percy family at the Battle of Shrewsbury in 1403 and was instrumental in putting down Owen Glendower's rebellion in Wales. As his father's health failed, Henry became increasingly prominent, for a time heading the council that ran the country in the king's name. Differences of opinion over policy led to Henry being dismissed from this post in 1411.

Succeeding his father in 1413, Henry V made a new start. Lords who had been out of favour under his father's rule were restored to former positions, and Richard II was laid to rest with honours suitable to his royal station. Henry made it clear that what had happened in his father's reign was in the past. In that, Henry V was forgiving, but not yielding. He crushed the Lollard religious movement even though its leader, John Oldcastle, was his friend. The result was a revolt and a plot against the king, from which Henry V emerged victorious.

With his position in England secure, Henry entered into negotiations with France. His chief bargaining points were the very large sum still owed from the ransom of King John II of France, captured by the English in 1356, and Henry's claim to

Left: Henry V attempted to resolve conflict with France through diplomacy, but when this failed he was quite willing to use more direct means. His invasion of France led to the great English victory at Agincourt.

THE SIEGE OF HARFLEUR LASTED A MONTH AND ENDED IN NEGOTIATED SURRENDER. ALTHOUGH COMBAT LOSSES WERE SMALL, THE ENGLISH ARMY BECAME AFFLICTED WITH DYSENTERY.

the French throne by way of descent from Edward III. Territorial exchanges and dynastic marriage were on the table, and a lasting settlement with France might actually have been possible. However, the French crown was not willing to pay the immense dowry Henry wanted; once diplomacy had failed, he made plans for invasion.

The campaign in France opened with a successful siege of Harfleur, after which Henry marched his army towards Calais. His force was suffering badly from disease as a result of the time spent besieging Harfleur, and was not in fighting condition when it was intercepted by the much larger French army under Charles d'Albret, Constable of France.

Badly outnumbered and certain to be outmanoeuvred by the French, whose main striking force was cavalry, Henry adopted

Below: The importance of archery at Agincourt is obvious from this depiction. Commonly, the great leaders would be in the centre or foreground, but here it is the common bowmen who take the centre stage.

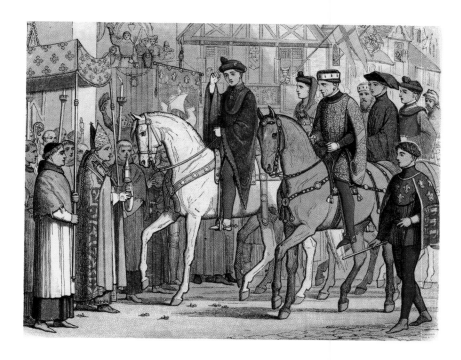

Left: Henry's campaigns in France led to the Treaty of Troyes, under whose terms Henry and his descendants would gain the throne of France upon the death of Charles VI.

a defensive stance. The French did likewise, trying to force the English to advance against them. In this they were partially successful. The English archers moved into shooting range and emplaced sharpened stakes to protect themselves before engaging the French host. The French sent cavalry at the archers, but their charges were repulsed in time for the English to turn their longbows against the main French force as it began to advance.

Woods on the flanks funnelled the French cavalry into a killing ground, and muddy conditions ensured they could not cross it quickly. As at Crécy and on other occasions, the longbows did great harm among the French, but did not prevent them from closing with the men-at-arms protecting the archers. Henry V distinguished himself in the hand-to-hand fighting that followed, and repeated attacks were repulsed by the hard-pressed English.

French losses at Agincourt were enormous, particularly among the nobility. Despite still having more troops on the field than the English, the French withdrew and Henry was able to complete his march to Calais. There was no prospect of doing more than reaching safety; Henry's army was in a terrible state and had to be satisfied with surviving the French onslaught.

Opposite: Henry VI came to the throne as a child and was wholly unsuited to rule England. Opposition to the increasing power of his favourites was one of the causes of the Wars of the Roses.

Although at the time Henry could not exploit his victory at Agincourt, his next campaign was highly successful. Realizing the importance of controlling the sea passages to and from the continent, Henry set about destroying or driving off the Genoese naval forces then in French service and establishing England as master of the Channel. In this, perhaps, can be seen the beginnings of British naval dominance.

A combination of deft political manoeuvring and opportunism – taking advantage of disputes between French nobles and allies – enabled Henry to capture Rouen and besiege Paris in 1419. The Treaty of Troyes the following year named Henry as regent of France and heir to its throne, solemnized by his marriage to Catherine, daughter of the French king. Catherine bore Henry a son – the future Henry VI – but with opposition remaining in France, he returned for another campaign. Henry was afflicted with dysentery at the Siege of Meaux and died in 1422, leaving an infant to become king of England.

THE IDEA OF NOBLES PICKING ROSES TO INDICATE THEIR LOYALTIES SEEMS TO HAVE ORIGINATED WITH SHAKESPEARE; THERE IS LITTLE EVIDENCE TO SUGGEST IT ACTUALLY HAPPENED.

WARS OF THE ROSES (1455–1485)

In the early medieval period, kings tended to be much more powerful than any of their subjects and could give whatever orders they pleased. As the nobles gained in power, this situation changed, forcing monarchs to bargain with their subjects or to scheme against them to maintain the power of the crown. The succession of Henry VI to the throne created an opportunity for the great nobility of England to advance their own positions by gaining control of the boy.

Ultimately, this led to the period known as the Wars of the Roses, after the white and red rose symbols of the main factions – the houses of York and Lancaster. In fact, the conflict was far more than a simple two-sided struggle, with many cross-cutting rivalries and semi-related disputes complicating an already difficult situation. The factional identities gradually faded as the wars went on, but at the beginning they were reasonably clear-

cut, with the Lancastrian faction in control of the capital and the king, and the Yorkists with a large but more dispersed power base.

The death of Henry V in 1422 placed his one-year-old son Henry on the throne at a time when England was embroiled in the Hundred Years' War. Henry V of England also became king of France soon afterwards, by way of inheritance from his grandfather Charles VI. This was disputed by the future Charles VII of France, and during Henry's reign almost all English holdings in France were lost.

Henry was by all accounts a kind and rather gentle man, better suited to be a priest than a ruler, and was unable to withstand the mental rigours of kingship. He had perhaps become used to allowing his great nobles to guide him during his childhood, when England was ruled by a council of regents, and was largely governed by his favourites. Meanwhile, Richard, Duke of York, was openly critical of Henry and his favourites. He was given the prestigious office of Lieutenant of Ireland largely to keep him away from court.

Richard of York returned from Ireland in the hope of remedying the situation in England, eventually leading to an armed standoff. Parlaying with the king, Richard convinced his Henry that he wanted only to set right what was going wrong in England. This included the king being under the sway of his favourites, who Richard considered were not acting in the best interests of Henry and his realm.

Although some minor readjustments took place at court, nothing really changed until 1453, when Henry VI suffered a mental breakdown upon hearing of defeat at the Battle of Castillon. Richard,

Duke of York, became regent in his name, but upon Henry's recovery he was once more eclipsed by Henry's favourites.

Hearing that King Henry had called a council to be held at Leicester, to which he and his allies were not invited, Richard of York realized he was about to be the victim of a political manoeuvre and tried to repeat his earlier gambit. Intercepting the royal contingent at St Albans before it could join with other forces, he hoped to make the king listen to him once again, but this time fighting broke out and the Royal army was defeated. It seems that Henry VI suffered another breakdown during the battle; he was captured while wandering around in a stupor.

CONFLICT BETWEEN THE YORKISTS AND THE KING'S FAVOURITES BEGAN ALMOST POLITELY, BUT ESCALATED INTO A SAVAGE AND BLOODY CIVIL WAR.

Richard of York once again became regent, this time with Henry VI imprisoned. Richard was surprisingly fair and lenient during his reign, permitting many of Henry's former favourites to hold high office and attempting to deal fairly with all concerned. In 1456, Henry regained his sanity once again and was returned to the throne. Richard of York went back to Ireland and very soon Henry was once more surrounded by favourites who moulded him to their ambitions.

The following year, the leaders of the Yorkist faction were summoned to a council by the king. Refusal to attend was treason, but Richard of York and his allies strongly suspected the intent was to separate them from their followers and arrest them. There was no alternative but armed resistance, and after early skirmishes the royal army marched on Ludlow Castle, where the Yorkists were mustering. This was a decisive moment, as up to this point Richard of York had not raised arms directly against the king. The battle at Ludlow was a disaster for the Yorkists, although their leaders escaped.

In 1459, the 'Parliament of Devils' passed a bill of attainder against the Yorkist leaders, declaring them traitors without the need for a trial. This was the point of no return; afterwards, the war took on an increasingly savage character. Richard of York went to Ireland to raise forces and Richard Neville, Earl of Warwick, did

Opposite: Richard of York was the chief opponent of the Lancastrian faction, though apparently a reluctant one. His governance as regent during the king's incapacity due to mental illness was fair and merciful.

the same at Calais. Warwick was able to raise a considerable force
for a joint expedition into England beginning in 1460.

Success in battle enabled the Yorkists to force an agreement
whereby Henry VI would rule for the remainder of his life, but
Richard of York would be his heir. This was not acceptable
to Henry's wife, Margaret of Anjou, who raised forces in the
north of England with help from the Scots. Richard of York was
defeated and killed, causing leadership of his faction to pass to
his son, the future Edward IV.

The Lancastrian force, under the command of Margaret of
Anjou, marched towards London to free the imprisoned King
Henry VI. This resulted in another battle at St Albans in which
King Henry, who was with the Yorkist army, was liberated. He
was at the time having another fit of madness, and was protected
by honourable Yorkist knights who were put to death despite
their chivalrous deed.

The Lancastrian force was not able to enter London, and
retired northwards. Meanwhile, Yorkist forces under Edward,
Earl of March, had defeated a Lancastrian army in a bloody
battle at Mortimer's Cross. A meteorological phenomenon before

the battle was taken as a good omen, and resulted in Edward taking 'the sunne in splendour' as his symbol. Edward joined forces with the defeated Yorkist force from St Albans at London, where he was crowned Edward IV in March 1461.

Another clash at Towdon resulted in very heavy casualties for the Lancastrian forces and gave Edward control of England. Henry VI and Margaret of Anjou found refuge in Scotland and continued to resist as best they could. Other Lancastrian leaders fled to the continent or surrendered, and Edward was surprisingly lenient towards them. Indeed, many were pardoned and offered important positions, which did not always reconcile them to Edward's rule. Some of the pardoned Lancastrians raised revolt against Edward; others gave good service in their new roles. Henry VI was eventually captured and once again imprisoned, although Edward appears to have treated him kindly.

THE EARL OF WARWICK PRESUMED TO MAKE ROYAL POLICY WITHOUT CONSULTING THE KING, AND EVENTUALLY TRIED TO TAKE CONTROL OF THE KINGDOM.

Having apparently consolidated his rule by the mid-1460s, Edward IV seemed to be in a good position. However, his ally Richard Neville, Earl of Warwick, overstepped his remit and began doing as he pleased, including opening negotiations with the French crown for a dynastic marriage between Edward and Anne of France. This clashed with Edward's plans for an alliance with Burgundy, and in any case was far beyond what he was empowered to do.

Edward IV married Elizabeth Woodville, daughter of a prominent Lancastrian commander, in 1464 and later entered into an alliance with Burgundy. This angered Warwick as it not only brought his plans for an alliance with France to nothing but also made him seem less than honest in his dealings with the French crown.

Opposite: Edward IV's marriage to Elizabeth Woodville alienated the powerful Earl of Warwick, and the elevation of her family to high positions caused great resentment among the nobility of England. This would ultimately lead to a new phase of the conflict.

The subsequent rapid rise of the Woodville family alienated other prominent nobles and brought about a new round of intrigues, including rebellions fomented by Warwick. It was in the course of putting down one such revolt that Edward IV was caught by a surprise invasion from the continent, led by Warwick himself, and was captured after a defeat at Edgecote.

This put Richard Neville, Earl of Warwick, in de facto control of England. He had two kings under his control – Edward IV and Henry VI – but released Edward to resume ruling subject to Warwick's conditions. Edward was able to reassert himself by 1470, so Warwick engineered another rebellion to draw the king out, intending to attack his army with forces ostensibly raised to help defeat the rebels. Edward crushed the rebellion far more quickly than expected, however, and obtained proof of Warwick's complicity as well as that of his own brother George, Duke of Clarence.

Warwick fled to the continent and made common cause with Margaret of Anjou. With the Duke of Clarence, Warwick landed in England and forced Edward IV to flee. He freed Henry VI and used him as a figurehead king, much to the disappointment of Clarence, who expected to be given the crown. Clarence offered to support his brother Edward if he attempted to retake the throne, and with assistance from Duke Charles of Burgundy he did so.

UNITED IN THEIR OPPOSITION TO EDWARD IV, FORMER LANCASTRIAN MARGARET OF ANJOU AND FORMER YORKIST WARWICK PLANNED A JOINT CAMPAIGN TO DEPOSE THE KING.

Edward landed in England in 1471, bringing about a decisive clash with Warwick's forces at Barnet. The right of Edward's force was commanded by Richard, Duke of Gloucester – the future Richard III. Warwick's army was crushed, and he was killed along with several other opponents of Edward, but on the very same day Margaret of Anjou and her bloodthirsty son Edward of Westminster landed in England.

Margaret had hoped to join forces with Warwick, but decided not to return to France even after learning of his defeat. Her army was caught by Edward's force near Tewkesbury and defeated. Edward of Westminster was captured and put to death and Margaret of Anjou was taken prisoner soon afterwards. Henry VI, still imprisoned, died under mysterious circumstances. It is possible that he was killed by Richard of Gloucester, although the official cause of death was 'melancholy'.

Stability gradually returned to England after 1471. Edward IV lived out the remainder of his reign in relative security, although he faced revolts, Scottish incursions and further plotting by his

brother the Duke of Clarence. He died in 1483, with his son
Edward as heir. The young Edward set off for London for his
coronation, and was met en route by Richard of Gloucester.
Richard was Edward's uncle and would be his regent and
protector until he came of age. The young Edward thus had no
reason to mistrust him.

Richard of Gloucester imprisoned Edward in the Tower of
London, although preparations for his coronation continued.
After a time, Edward's younger brother was persuaded to join
him, and the two met a mysterious fate that has been the subject
of much speculation ever since. In the meantime, Richard
concocted a rather spurious case for Edward and his brother to
be illegitimate, making their claim to the throne invalid, and had
himself crowned Richard III of England.

Below: Richard Neville,
Earl of Warwick,
played a central role in
the Wars of the Roses
until he was killed in
battle at Barnet. The
battle was fought
in misty conditions,
which contributed to
Warwick's defeat.

In 1483, Richard faced a rebellion led by the Duke of
Buckingham, which was supposed to coincide with the landing
of Henry Tudor from the continent. Henry was a distant relative
of the royal family, whose blood claim to the throne was so thin
that even amid the savagery of the Wars of the Roses he was not
executed when captured at Pembroke Castle as a young child.

Henry Tudor was delayed, and Buckingham's rebellion
collapsed. When Henry did begin his campaign, he received

support from disaffected nobles in England and Wales, but would be greatly outnumbered if he allowed Richard III to gather his forces. He therefore staked everything on a decisive battle, which occurred at Bosworth in 1485.

The outcome was decided as much by politics as fighting power. Part of Richard's army declined to join the fighting, making it likely that he would be defeated. Richard therefore took a gamble of his own, charging with his retinue directly at

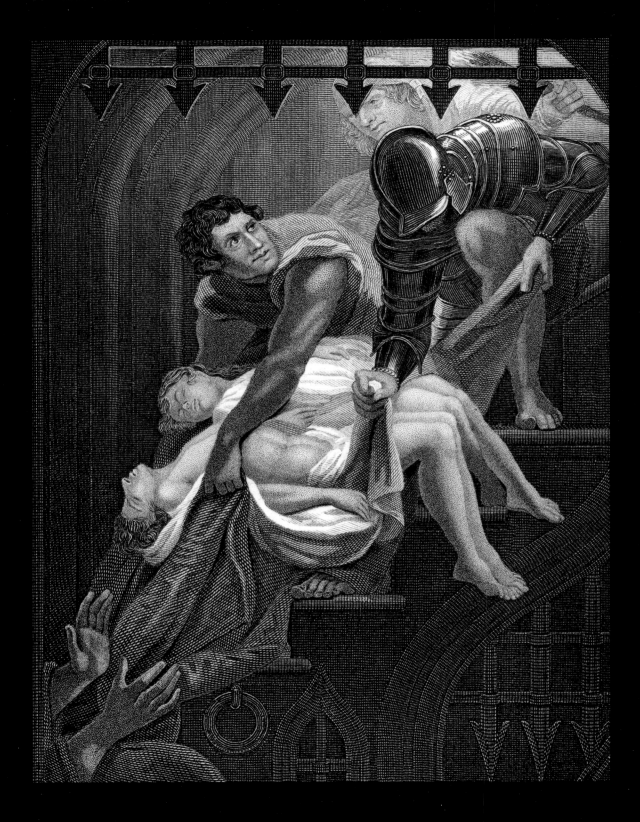

Henry Tudor's escort. According to some accounts, Richard fought Henry Tudor directly, and certainly his force came close to killing Henry and perhaps causing his army to collapse. Ultimately, however, Richard's bold gambit failed. Far from calling for a horse to flee the battle as Shakespeare portrayed, Richard III refused the offer of a mount and stayed on the field until he was killed.

This left Henry Tudor as the final victor in the Wars of the Roses. He was crowned king of England as Henry VII and consolidated his position despite a weak blood claim. Rebellions and conflict with Scotland did not greatly threaten Henry's reign, and his marriage to Elizabeth of York legitimized his claim to the throne as well as uniting what remained of the Yorkist and Lancastrian factions. The Wars of the Roses can be considered the last great medieval conflict in Western Europe, and Henry's assumption of the throne in many ways marked the end of an era.

Opposite: The story of the 'princes in the tower' continues to attract interest and controversy today. Richard III is accused of having them murdered, though there is no proof either way.

Below: Richard III's defeat at the Battle of Bosworth brought the Wars of the Roses to an end. Richard died trying to wrest victory from defeat by sheer force of arms.

2

CRUSADERS, PERSECUTORS AND RELIGIOUS REFORMERS

Religion, and conflict between religious groups, was a driving force in the statecraft of the Middle Ages. Religion was a tool of politics and vice versa. The favour of the Pope could sway an issue one way or the other; winning it often required furthering the cause of the Church either by internal actions or by participating in a crusade.

EXCOMMUNICATION WAS a powerful weapon in the hands of the Pope, used as a threat or a punishment. Excommunication of a ruler extended to his whole realm, and fear for their souls was a powerful factor in sowing discontent among the populace. Thus, the displeasure of the Pope was not just a spiritual problem – it could destabilize an otherwise peaceful realm.

Many of the most prominent rulers of the Middle Ages won fame on crusade. For others, crusading was a necessary factor

Opposite: The entry of the Crusaders into Constantinople. Whilst the event occurred during the Fourth Crusade, it is viewed through the lens of mid-19th Century Romanticism.

Below: Louis the Pious may have allowed his religious fervour to outweigh his duties. He made the grave mistake of apologising for his actions, suggesting to his enemies that he was weak.

in avoiding the consequences of earlier actions; in some cases, it seems to have been something of an obsession. Some rulers allowed themselves to be distracted from real problems at home by their adventures in the Holy Land or in Spain.

There were other religious factors at play as well. The status of Jews in medieval Europe was prone to change from tolerance to oppression and murder almost overnight, and the rise of various heresies – at least as defined by the mainstream Church – could have political ramifications. Approval by the Church created a convenient 'us and them' situation: conflict between Christian states was generally discouraged by the Pope, with those of a combative nature directed towards fighting outsiders such as heretics, pagans and the Islamic states. Similarly, tolerance towards a heresy, or support of the 'wrong' sect, might result in a ruler being the target of a crusade within Europe.

Some religious figures were also prone to take a political stance that was not to the liking of their king, leading to internal conflict. This was an era where high church office might be awarded for political reasons and – in some realms at least – religious posts were given to favourites as a reward for loyalty, bringing additional wealth and power.

LOUIS THE PIOUS (814–840)
Champion of Western Christianity
Louis was the third son of Charlemagne, behind Charles and Pepin. All three were well educated and trained to lead Frankish forces in war, but only Louis outlived his father. As was the custom of the time, each of Charles' sons was designated to be ruler of a part of the overall Frankish kingdom; Louis received Aquitaine and spent much of his youth there. Charles was to be Emperor and rule Francia, while Pepin would receive Italy as king of the Lombards.

Long before becoming a ruler in his own right, Louis campaigned in Spain and Italy on behalf of his father. After the deaths of his brothers – Pepin probably from a fever contracted at the Siege of Venice in 810 and Charles from a stroke in 811 – Louis was crowned co-emperor with his father in 813.

Charlemagne enjoyed good health until the last four years of his life, dying in 814. From him, Louis inherited an all-but-unified Europe and the possibility of creating a lasting empire. He began his reign by destroying pagan texts and sending those members of the court whose religious fervour was in doubt to be confined in monasteries and nunneries. This included members of his own family, and was intended as much to remove them from politics as to punish their lack of faith. Nonetheless, papal approval was forthcoming and in 816 Louis was crowned a second time – on this occasion by Pope Stephen IV at Reims.

Hoping to ensure a clear succession, and in accordance with Frankish tradition, Louis issued instructions in 817 as to how his empire was to be divided among his three sons. Lothair, the eldest, was crowned as co-emperor and would inherit the Frankish heartland as well as the title of emperor and the

THE FRANKISH PRACTICE OF THE TIME WAS TO SUBDIVIDE THE EMPIRE BETWEEN SONS OF THE CURRENT RULER, WITH ONE RULING OVER THE OTHERS.

Above: Louis' second coronation, by Pope Stephen IV, assured the Franks that their ruler was righteous as well as mighty.

allegiance of his brothers. Pepin was to be king of Aquitaine, while his younger brother Louis received Bavaria.

LVDOVVICVS LOTHARI⁹
R·EX   R·EX

Above: Louis' sons Lothair and Louis, depicted as kings of Francia and Bavaria. Lothair was elevated above his brothers as emperor, but each enjoyed considerable autonomy in his own realm.

While this decree created a clear-cut situation for Louis' sons, it had the opposite effect for his nephew Bernard, who had inherited the crown of Italy from his father, Louis' brother Pepin. Bernard began moving towards independence from Louis' empire, but faced a swift and decisive response from Louis. Surrendering, Bernard was sentenced to death for treason. Although his sentence was commuted to blinding, he died anyway.

Louis was filled with remorse over Bernard's death, and made public penance. This may have salved his own conscience, but in an era where a ruler had to be above all else strong, he undermined his own position by appearing too apologetic for his actions. Similarly, while his strong support for the Church – notably laws protecting Church property – won him favour in that quarter, Louis was not as well regarded as a warrior.

This perceived weakness in war led to Louis having to fight far more than might otherwise have been necessary. Tribes along the frontiers, who had initially been intimidated by Frankish power, began to rebel. Louis launched a successful campaign against Slavic tribes in Pannonia and Bulgaria, and later attempted to pacify southern Italy. Lasting success eluded Louis in the East, and expeditions into Spain against the Cordoban Caliphate were equally unsuccessful.

Internal conflict characterized the reign of Louis, not least due to the birth of a fourth son, Charles, to his second wife. Seeking to secure an appropriate inheritance for Charles, Louis decided to redistribute the previously assigned inheritances. This caused anger and resentment, which in 830 spilled over into civil war. Returning from a campaign in the east, Louis marched into a confused situation and was captured by his sons. A round of bargaining and offers of greater inheritance divided the sons, resulting in Louis being freed and receiving their renewed loyalty.

Two years later, Louis' sons again rebelled against him, and much of his army deserted. This may have been the result of Pope Gregory IV speaking out against Louis, but whatever the reason he decided to spare his remaining loyal supporters a hopeless battle. Louis was deposed for a time, but bickering among his sons allowed him to return to the throne in time to meet a large-scale Viking incursion in 837.

A third civil war began in 839, resulting from Louis' redistribution of territories among whichever of his sons was not in revolt at the time. Further incursions by the Norsemen complicated the situation, but with the assistance of his formerly rebellious son Lothair, Louis was able to restore stability to his empire by early 840. It was not to last, however. In June of that year Louis died and civil war once more tore apart the Frankish empire. It was not reunited, and in this split lay the beginnings of modern France and Germany, and of disputes over the territories in between.

Below: The death of Louis the Pious in 840 brought to an end the era of a unified Europe under Frankish rule.

FREDERICK I BARBAROSSA, HOLY ROMAN EMPEROR (1122–1190)

Leader of the Third Crusade

The First Crusade began in 1095, in response to a request for assistance from the Byzantine Emperor against Islamic encroachment. The campaign was a success, resulting in the capture of Jerusalem by crusader forces. Having set up crusader states at Edessa, Tripoli, Antioch and Jerusalem, most of the European force returned home.

By 1144, the crusader-held County of Edessa had fallen to the forces of Imad ad-Din Zengi, resulting in a new call for a crusade. This was led by Louis VII of France and Conrad III of Germany, who was accompanied by his nephew Frederick. Frederick had just become Duke of Swabia upon his father's death and emerged with his reputation intact from a campaign that ultimately ended in disaster.

At the time, Swabia was one of more than a thousand states (some of them extremely small) that made up Germany. A candidate for king had to be acceptable to the princes of these states – or at least not too objectionable. Frederick was an adept diplomat, typically appealing to the German princes' self-interest rather than trying to ram his new authority down their throats. His approach worked, and he was crowned king of Germany.

In accordance with a treaty of 1153 and in return for military assistance, the Pope crowned Frederick Barbarossa in 1155, but by 1158 they were at odds. Frederick, naturally,

Below: The Kyffhauser Monument in Thuringia includes this sandstone figure of Frederick Barbarossa. It refers to the legend that the emperor is sleeping under the nearby mountain and will awaken when a threat emerges.

felt that the Pope should be subordinate to the Holy Emperor, while the Pope was of the opinion that the Emperor should be a servant of the Church. Frederick launched a military campaign into Italy, and the newly appointed Pope Alexander III responded by excommunicating him.

Frederick Barbarossa's campaigns in Italy were locally successful at times, but the overall political situation did not allow him to assert his authority as he had hoped. As time went on, his excommunication began to have adverse effects on the stability of Germany, with revolts in some provinces and clergy openly speaking out against their Holy Emperor. Another campaign, this time against the Lombard League of northern Italy, was initially successful, but Frederick's army was defeated at the Battle of Legnago in 1176.

Frederick made peace with the Church and was no longer an excommunicate, but he continued to undermine the Pope's authority with political machinations. His son Henry married Constance, queen of Sicily, in 1186, gaining the title king of Italy. Frederick's plans were interrupted by the Pope's call for a third crusade, and, while Philip of France and Richard of England travelled by sea, Frederick's larger army marched towards the Holy Land.

Frederick Barbarossa is credited with leading an immense force on the Third Crusade, although there is much doubt about the actual number of troops he raised. Along the way he managed to recruit additional crusaders, notably in Hungary, but he faced opposition from the Byzantine emperor. Relations between Western crusaders and Byzantium had always been tricky, and were at times hostile. The first crusade was launched in response to a Byzantine request

Above: Frederick Barbarossa's Italian ambitions came to an end in 1176 with defeat at the Battle of Legnago. His opponents, the Lombard League, represented the last coherent military opposition to Frederick's campaign in Italy.

REJECTING AN OFFER OF SAFE PASSAGE IN RETURN FOR PAYMENT, FREDERICK BARBAROSSA INSTEAD DECLARED HE WOULD OPEN THE WAY WITH IRON.

Above: Victory at Iconium in 1190 was hard won, but opened the way for Frederick's crusaders to reach the Holy Land. Despite causing Saladin great alarm the crusade petered out after the death of Frederick.

Opposite: This depiction of the death of Frederick gives his end a heroic and dramatic aspect, whereas in truth it was most likely an unfortunate accident or the result of his declining health.

for assistance against Islamic encroachment, but at the end of the campaign land that had been recovered was not returned to Byzantium. Instead, it formed the basis of the crusader states in the Holy Land, a bone of contention thereafter.

Frederick Barbarossa then had to march his army through the territory of the Seljuk Turks, who offered safe passage in return for gold. Frederick is said to have retorted that he would instead open the road with iron, which proved to be a difficult undertaking. Although Frederick's crusaders won victories, they were constantly harassed on the march. Making slow progress and suffering steady casualties, the crusaders became dispirited, but had no choice but to keep going.

Reaching Iconium, Frederick at last succeeded in bringing the main Turkish army to battle. Victory allowed a siege of the city to begin, and in due course it fell. In the meantime, the Turks offered battle a second time and were again defeated. The capture of Iconium allowed Frederick to rest his army, after which the march was resumed.

As his army made a crossing of the River Saleph, Frederick died under circumstances that remain unclear. He may have drowned, although some sources suggest he suffered heart failure – he was nearly 70 at the time. It was hoped to take Frederick Barbarossa's body to Jerusalem, but even pickled in vinegar it began to decay rapidly. Instead, his remains were conveyed to Antioch, Tarsus and Tyre, and the German contingent abandoned their part in the crusade.

THE HOLY ROMAN EMPIRE

THE TERM 'Holy Roman Empire' was not used in the time of Frederick Barbarossa. Indeed, it was he that first referred to a *Sacrum Imperium* (Holy Empire). The empire had existed since the 800s under various titles, and was at times considered, in spirit at least, to be a continuation of the Roman Empire. Roman connotations were dropped early on, but the word 'Roman' was added to the title in the 1200s.

Falling somewhere between political alliance and religious institution, the Holy Roman Empire included states in Italy and Germany. These were not ruled directly by the emperor any more than the territories of the princes of Germany were ruled by their king. However, the emperor was crowned by the Pope and wielded the collective power of the member states, making him one of the most important men in Europe.

The Holy Roman Emperor and the Pope at times disagreed as to whether the empire's legitimacy came from political reality or divine approval, although the truth lay somewhere in between. At times extremely powerful, the empire eventually waned in importance. By the end of the medieval period it was little more than a confederation of German states, although the empire existed at least in name until 1806.

Left: Frederick Barbarossa was required to make public submission to the Pope in order to be crowned Holy Emperor. However, he worked to undermine the Pope's authority and to assert himself instead.

HENRY II OF ENGLAND (1133–1189)

Challenged Church authority in England

The future Henry II was born in 1133, two years before the death of his grandfather Henry I. Henry I named his daughter, the empress Matilda (Henry's mother), as his successor, but the throne was seized instead by Count Stephen of Blois. The young Henry's early life was set against the backdrop of the Anarchy, as the struggle between Stephen and Matilda was known.

Henry took over from his mother in 1148, eventually resulting in an agreement that Stephen would remain on the throne until his death and be succeeded by Henry. By the time Stephen died in 1154, Henry had inherited Anjou and Normandy, and married Eleanor of Aquitaine. He was given various nicknames, including Curtmantle, but his dynasty became known as Plantagenet, from the French for a sprig of broom – the crest of the house of Anjou.

Henry II's reign was characterized by conflict with Philip II Augustus of France, who attempted to gain control over parts of Henry's 'Angevin Empire' in France. He also intervened in Ireland, attempting to put a puppet high king on the throne,

Above: Henry II's early life was overshadowed by war between his mother, the Empress Matilda, and Count Stephen of Blois who had seized the throne of England. Much of his early reign was spent repairing the damage resulting from this conflict.

Above: Henry II possessed immense territories in Britain and France, bringing with them an array of troubles ranging from tension with the French king to internal revolts and a difficult relationship with the Church.

after sweeping through Wales and suppressing rebellion there. However, Henry's first task upon ascending the throne was of setting his own house in order.

Henry set about repairing some of the damage caused by the Anarchy. In addition to measures aimed at restoring confidence in the currency, he reformed the way legal proceedings were conducted and established a system of courts and prisons. In this work, Henry was assisted by Thomas Becket (1118–1170), who had previously served the Archbishop of Canterbury. As Henry's chancellor, Becket proved an able supporter. He was rewarded with the office of Archbishop of Canterbury when the previous incumbent, Theobald, died in 1161.

Although Henry and Becket had been friends, they found themselves increasingly at odds as Henry tried to control the Church. Becket was willing to oppose such moves and to ensure his subordinates did likewise. He was at times rather liberal in his use of excommunication against Henry's supporters, and was forced to flee to France in 1164. Negotiations were attempted, since Henry wanted Becket to crown his eldest son as co-ruler, but this came to nothing. Becket placed an interdict on England resulting in a new round of negotiations, and he resumed his post in late 1170.

Conflict between Henry II and Becket continued, with more excommunications, until Henry voiced his frustration with his archbishop. According to popular legend, Henry burst out, 'Will no-one rid me of this turbulent priest?' although there are several versions of this tale. Be that as it may, four of Henry's knights decided to arrest Becket. He resisted, believing they had no authority to do so, and they dealt with the problem in the most extreme manner.

Henry had five sons by Eleanor of Aquitaine, although the eldest, William, did not survive childhood. Henry decided to crown his next son during his own lifetime in accordance with an old Frankish tradition. Henry the Young King, as he became known, died in 1183 aged 28 and did not succeed his father. In the meantime, Henry became increasingly estranged from Eleanor of Aquitaine and faced rebellions from his remaining sons. Most notable among these was the Great Revolt of 1173–74, which may have been instigated by Eleanor herself. Eleanor was imprisoned thereafter, for the remainder of Henry's reign.

Below: The killing of Thomas Becket probably arose from an attempt on his part to face down a group of Henry's knights whose authority he chose not to recognize.

Below: Eleanor of Aquitaine was a formidable and powerful woman, who was initially a valuable supporter of Henry II. Their increasing estrangement led to her being imprisoned.

Henry's fourth son, Geoffrey, died in 1186. This left Henry with two possible heirs: Richard and his favourite, John. Philip of France used the disaffection of Henry's sons to his own advantage, allying with Richard against his father in the last months of Henry's life. One bone of contention between Richard and his father was the coming Third Crusade. Both Henry and Philip had declared their intention to take part, and Richard was particularly eager, but a number of issues between England and France had to be settled first.

Richard's impatience was exploited by Philip, until in late 1188 Richard openly declared allegiance to the French king. John joined Richard in revolt, but Henry was already too ill to fight. After agreeing a settlement with Philip that was little short of abject surrender, Henry retired to his ancestral lands in Anjou where he died soon afterwards.

RICHARD I (THE LIONHEART) OF ENGLAND (1157–1199)

Crusader first, king second

Richard was the son of Henry II of England and Eleanor of Aquitaine. He was born in England, but as his parents' relationship cooled he went with his mother to her home duchy, where he was raised. Richard was his mother's favourite son; his younger brother, John, was favoured by their father. This may have been a factor in his decision to join his older brother Henry the Young King in revolt against their father.

The revolt of 1173 was a serious threat to Henry II, but afterwards he and Richard were reconciled, and Richard fought against Henry the Young King during his next revolt in 1183. Richard was named his father's heir – he had already been promised Aquitaine by his mother – but was increasingly at odds with his father after 1184. Indeed, at the time of Henry II's death in 1189 Richard was in revolt against him.

One of the reasons for contention between Richard and his father had been Richard's desire to go on crusade. The capture of Jerusalem in 1187 by Saladin resulted in calls for a new crusade to retake it, and Richard was keen to participate.

Richard found his father's reluctance to put the affairs of England second to the call of the crusade inconvenient, and as relations soured he chose to side with Philip of France. This was not the betrayal it might seem to the modern observer; many English nobles had holdings in France and were therefore vassals of the French crown as well as that of England.

Negotiations broke down, and Richard sided with Philip to attack his father, who was at the time gravely ill. Henry II died during the campaign, and Richard was successful in pressing his claim to the throne of England. He was surprisingly lenient towards his father's supporters, even those who had stood against him, and quickly had his mother released from her imprisonment.

Richard also arranged for his half-brother, Geoffrey Plantagenet, to become Archbishop of York – a role for which he was entirely unsuited. Geoffrey shared his half-brother's volatile temperament and was soon at odds with the Pope. Refusing to go to Rome to explain himself, Geoffrey asked Richard to intercede for him, but somehow managed to turn a request for assistance into a diatribe on Richard's sins. This drove Richard into a rage, and resulted in Geoffrey being dismissed from his post.

Richard's journey to the Holy Land was eventful. The joint English-French force led by Richard and Philip II of France went first to Sicily, where they liberated Richard's recently widowed sister Joanna from imprisonment by Tancred, new king of Sicily. Although successful in forcing Tancred to release Joanna and compensate her for her lost inheritance, events in Sicily showed the beginnings of a rift between Richard and Philip.

RICHARD I WAS INVOLVED IN SEVERAL REVOLTS AGAINST HIS FATHER, AT TIMES IN OPEN ALLIANCE WITH PHILIP AUGUSTUS OF FRANCE.

Below: Richard I is generally depicted in a positive light in Britain, despite having neglected his responsibilities as king in order to fulfil his crusading ambitions. His total time spent in England can be measured in weeks.

Tension was increased by Richard's announcement that he intended to wed Berengaria of Navarre, as he had previously been betrothed to Philip's daughter Alys. Berengaria and Joanna were then shipwrecked on Cyprus and taken prisoner. Richard's forces conquered the island and freed the captives along with large sums of money captured with them. Richard and Berengaria were married on Cyprus and she accompanied him on campaign for a short time before departing homeward.

The conquest of Cyprus, unintended as it had been, gave the crusaders a useful base close to the Holy Land and also raised Richard's status as a military leader. Indeed, when his forces landed at Acre in 1191, the defenders were keen to surrender the city. Richard's temper caused further rifts between himself and Philip of France, and also with Leopold V of Austria, who led a German force. In addition to personal insults, Leopold suspected Richard of being implicated in the death of Conrad of Montferrat, who had just been elected king of Jerusalem by the crusaders.

Philip II withdrew from the crusade and returned to France, while Richard marched on Arsuf with his army. There he won a notable victory despite the superior mobility of Saladin's forces. Among Richard's achievements was persuading his knights to hold back their headlong charge until the moment was exactly right, allowing footsoldiers to take the brunt of the enemy attacks.

Despite this victory, the crusaders did not manage to take Jerusalem, and Richard was forced to conclude a truce with Saladin in order to deal with problems at home. His brother John, he learned, had allied himself with Philip of France, who was seeking to annex some of Richard's French holdings.

Left: Richard's victory at Arsuf was a triumph of discipline in the face of great adversity. It required holding back the normally impetuous Crusader cavalry until their charge would be most effective.

ALTHOUGH DUKE LEOPOLD WAS THE SENIOR GERMAN CRUSADER IN THE EXPEDITION, RICHARD DID NOT CONSIDER HIM A PEER.

Opposite: There is no doubt that Richard I was an effective military leader, but his interactions with other rulers were difficult.

Richard sailed for England, but was forced ashore by bad weather and captured by Leopold V of Austria. Leopold had a personal grudge against Richard, and was quite happy to receive a king's ransom. He was also offered additional funds from France to hold Richard captive a little longer.

After his release in 1194, Richard was reconciled with his brother John and named him heir, spending the next five years resisting French pressure against his holdings on the continent. He was mortally wounded at the siege of Chalus in 1199 and died soon afterwards, having spent very little time in his realm of England. Indeed, Richard seems to have viewed England more as a source of funds for his crusading than a realm to be governed. Likewise, he spent little time with his wife Berengaria and did not produce a legitimate heir.

Richard's career furthered the reputation of English kings as great warriors, and perhaps advanced the crusader cause

Below: On his deathbed, Richard forgave the crossbowman who mortally wounded him and promised leniency. Accounts vary, but it seems his promise was not kept; the crossbowman was put to a gruesome death.

somewhat by the capture of Cyprus. He is notable for his adoption of the phrase 'Dieu et mon Droit' ('God and my right'), which has been the motto of the English crown ever since.

LOUIS IX OF FRANCE (SAINT LOUIS) (1214–1270)

Statesman, crusader and reformer

Louis VIII of France had an eventful career despite dying relatively young, aged 39. In addition to inheriting the throne of France from Philip II, Louis VIII also became – albeit very briefly and unofficially – king of England. In his youth, Louis VIII was invited to take the crown of England by barons who were in rebellion against King John. Later, he conducted a successful campaign against the French holdings of the English crown and joined the Albigensian Crusade against the Cathar sect in France.

Louis IX came to the throne in 1226 at the age of 12, upon the death of his father, Louis VIII. His mother, Blanche of Castile, acted as regent during his youth. Blanche was successful in dealing with the inevitable power plays surrounding a very young king, with the result that Louis took up the reins of a stable realm in 1234. During his career he proved to be an adept statesman, willing to renounce his own territorial claims in return for the same from his rivals. In this way he steadily reduced the level of threat to his realm.

Above: Louis IX was a wise ruler who worked towards removing the causes of future conflict. The agreements he negotiated resolved numerous causes of friction long before they could escalate into conflict.

Stability did not equate to the total absence of conflict, of course. Louis faced a serious challenge in 1242 when Henry III of England invaded France in support of a revolt by Hugh of Lusignan, receiving considerable support from the French nobility. Louis disposed of this threat with a victory at Taillebourg. With the situation at home reasonably secure, he began preparations to go on crusade. His reasons were in part personal; he felt that his recovery from a serious illness was miraculous, and wanted to show his gratitude. There were also

Above: The Seventh Crusade was intended to seize territory, which could be used in subsequent negotiations rather than making a head-on assault on the Holy Land. Ironically, Louis' greatest contribution to the Crusader cause came after his defeat.

political factors; the situation was worsening for the crusader kingdoms of the Holy Land, and Louis wanted to assist them before it was too late.

Louis thus took the cross and led a large force on the Seventh Crusade, beginning in 1248. Whereas the first crusades had taken the form of a straightforward campaign into the Holy Land with the intention of capturing key cities or destroying enemy armies, later crusades were often convoluted affairs with bargains and favours required to obtain cooperation or transport. Crusader armies at times acted as mercenaries in the service of those from whom they wanted assistance, expending their energies on targets that had nothing to do with fighting Islam or taking control of the Holy Land.

Louis' plan was to invade Egypt rather than the Holy Land, capturing territory that could be used as bargaining chips in negotiations for the surrender of cities taken by Muslim forces. At first the campaign went well, but, worn down by the rigours of war and by plague, the crusader army was eventually forced to withdraw. Louis and many of his knights were captured during the retreat. Once ransomed, Louis proceeded to the Holy Land rather than return home in defeat, and managed to improve the situation there through adept diplomacy. He returned to France upon receiving news of his mother's death. Blanche of Castile had been acting as regent in Louis' absence, so a speedy return was now vital.

Even before his diplomatic successes in Syria, Louis was well regarded for many reasons. He was renowned as a fair and just man who made many progressive reforms. He ended the practice of trial by combat or ordeal – essentially based on the idea that God would protect an innocent from fire, boiling water or the weapons of an opponent – and implemented the presumption of innocence in legal proceedings.

Louis' administrative reforms included measures to protect confidence in coinage and rules to guide the affairs of royal officials and clergymen. Profiteering and corruption were perks of the job for many administrators in the realms of Europe; forcing his officials to deal more honestly increased Louis' popularity

Below: Louis' army landed in Egypt and quickly captured the port of Damietta. Despite possessing a secure base, the crusade became bogged down by siege warfare and the flooding of the Nile, and was ultimately defeated at the Battle of Fariksur.

LOUIS IX PASSED LAWS TO
REGULATE THE CONDUCT OF
OFFICIALS, REDUCING CORRUPTION
AND INCREASING HIS POPULARITY.

with the folk of France. Some of his reforms
straddled the line between law and religion,
such as laws against prostitution, blasphemy
and gambling.

Louis took advantage of the opportunity
to buy a collection of holy relics, adding more
later. To house them he built the great chapel of Sainte-Chapelle
in Paris, one of several prominent buildings he had constructed.
Given the weakness of the Holy Roman Emperor at the time,
Louis was regarded as the foremost ruler of Christendom, and
may have had ambitions to replace the emperor.

In 1269, Louis began preparations for a new crusade, this
time to north Africa. He landed in Tunisia and was initially
successful, but died of plague in 1270. His army returned home
with his body, to great shows of public respect and sorrow. Louis
IX was popularly acclaimed as a saint by his people, and in 1297
the Pope formally canonized him.

Below: Louis IX
considered his recovery
from a bout of serious
illness to be miraculous,
but this did not prevent
him from suffering from
dysentery on the Seventh
Crusade and again, this
time fatally, on the Eighth.

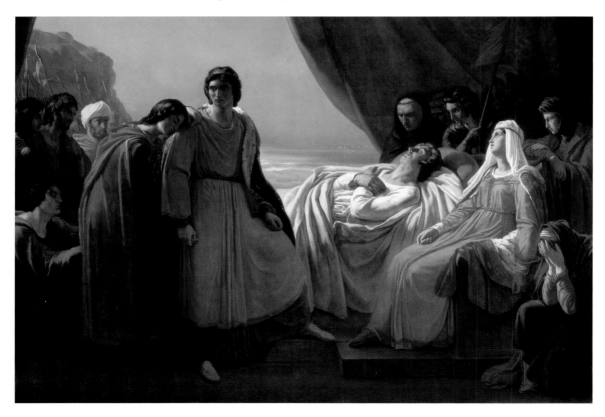

THE JUDICIAL DUEL

THE JUDICIAL DUEL, or trial by combat, was typically a Germanic tradition, although it was also practised by the Franks. Much of the time the combat was between reasonably well matched opponents. It was not uncommon for the great nobility to use champions to settle their disputes, but ordinary folk were also tried by combat. Surviving *fechtbücher* ('fighting manuals') from the 1400s depict the arrangements for a duel between a husband and wife, giving advice on how to make the duel a fair fight and how each combatant might go about winning it.

Judicial duels continued to occur from time to time after Louis' ban, and were sometimes bizarre. The behaviour of a greyhound – normally a gentle and friendly animal – owned by a missing nobleman towards one of his associates was taken as an accusation. The dog, having witnessed the murder of its master, was able to lead investigators to a shallow grave where the body had been hidden. At the subsequent duel, the dog mauled the murderer, effectively proving its case, and extracted a confession that led to a sentence of death by hanging.

Below: The idea of the judicial duel was that God would give victory to the party who was in the right. Similarly, trial by ordeal assumed that an innocent would be protected or divinely healed of injuries.

SIGISMUND VON LUXEMBOURG, HOLY ROMAN EMPEROR (1368–1437)

Leader of the last Crusade

Sigismund's grandfather was John of Luxembourg (later known as John the Blind), who married Elizabeth of Bohemia. He was not popular in his new home country, and spent much of his time elsewhere. John had strong links with France, and along with his son Charles he fought at the Battle of Crécy in 1346. John was blind by this time, and was guided by a party of his knights.

John's death at Crécy placed his son Charles on the throne of Bohemia. Charles was the nephew of Charles IV of France, and spent several years at the French court. He assisted his father in governance before becoming king himself – king of Bohemia and later Burgundy and Italy as well. He was crowned Holy Roman Emperor in 1365.

Charles died in 1378, and Sigismund inherited the title of Margrave of Brandenburg while still a boy. He had been betrothed to Mary, daughter of King Louis of Hungary, since they were both small children, and had immersed himself in Hungarian culture at Louis' court. At the behest of his half-brother King Wenceslas of Germany and Bohemia, Sigismund was sent to Poland in 1381. He remained enmeshed in the affairs of Poland for the remainder of his career, benefiting greatly from acting as a mediator.

Below: Sigismund faced internal troubles as well as constant pressure from the Turks. Despite a weak position and lack of funds, he was eventually able to secure and even expand his holdings.

Louis of Bohemia died in 1382. Mary was crowned queen, and immediately faced resistance from elements of the nobility who wanted a male monarch. Charles III of Naples made a successful bid for the Hungarian crown, but was deposed and killed in 1386. Sigismund's marriage to Mary did not end the troubles surrounding the crown, but the nobility got the male ruler they wanted and Mary was relegated to the role of consort. She died after a fall from her horse in 1395 while pregnant. Her child, who would have been Sigismund's heir, did not survive.

Sigismund's reign was troubled. His position was weakened by financial problems and opposition from the nobility of his realm. Sigismund had to resort to bargaining with his vassals, giving away some of his lands in return for money or support. His control over Hungary remained tenuous for many years, and there were external problems as well. Notably this was due to the encroachments of the Ottoman Empire, but the situation in Poland was also difficult. King Louis had been king of Poland as well as Hungary, but, lacking a male heir, the crown passed to his daughter Jadwiga, sister of Mary.

Jadwiga married Grand Duke Jogaila of Lithuania, creating a powerful union between the two realms. However, although Jogaila had Christianized Lithuania, the Teutonic Order was not convinced of his sincerity. Sigismund was at times able to mediate in these affairs – sometimes to his own advantage – but Poland-Lithuania faced a crusade by the Teutonic knights, and its troubles spilled over into Hungary.

In 1396, ongoing conflict with the Turks resulted in the Pope calling for a crusade. Sigismund led the Christian army as far as Nicopolis, where it was defeated by a large force under Sultan Bayezid I, who had been besieging Constantinople. The crusade

Above: The marriage of Jadwiga of Poland to Jogaila of Lithuania created a powerful state, but resulted in conflict with the Teutonic Order.

Above: The Battle of
Nicopolis was a confused
and disjointed affair,
at least on the crusaders'
side. Crushing defeat
brought about the
end of the last major
attempt to contain
Turkish expansion.

failed to relieve Constantinople but may have weakened the siege; Bayezid withdrew in 1402 to deal with other threats.

Sigismund had a narrow escape at Nicopolis, but managed to return home. Hungary was highly unstable at the time, but despite the troubles of his kingdom Sigismund was able to exert and expand his authority. By 1433 he was Holy Roman Emperor and king of Germany and Bohemia. The latter crown was gained upon the death of his brother Wenceslas of Bohemia, whose demise was a factor in escalating the Hussite Wars.

Sigismund was a staunch opponent of the Hussites, who he denounced as heretics. For their part, the Hussites blamed Sigismund for betraying their founder, Jan Hus, who was burned at the stake despite a safe conduct guaranteed by Sigismund. The Hussites would not acknowledge Sigismund as king, and since they controlled large parts of Hungary they essentially deprived him of his realm. Sigismund led repeated campaigns against the Hussites until a negotiated settlement, known as the Compacta of Prague, was agreed in 1433. Once this had passed into law, Sigismund could finally be crowned in Bohemia.

In the meantime, Hungary was still under threat from the Turks, whose campaigns distracted Sigismund from his wars against the Hussites. Turkish pressure was also responsible for reducing the level of support that might otherwise have been available for the anti-Hussite crusades. Sigismund created a knightly order, the Order of the Dragon, to fight against Turkish incursions. However, his most notable achievement was his part in ending the Western Schism.

With two rival Popes, one in Italy and one in France, the Church was divided – a situation made worse by the emergence of a third Pope. As protector of the Church, Sigismund was instrumental in bringing about the Council of Constance, which finally resolved the question of papal legitimacy. He was less effective in protecting Jan Hus, who was arrested despite Sigismund's safe conduct and subsequently burned at the stake for heresy.

Sigismund died in 1437. His first marriage had produced no surviving children, and his second marriage resulted in a daughter who became Elizabeth of Bohemia. She was relegated to the role of consort when her husband was crowned, and his death in 1439 resulted in conflict over succession and a new civil war.

SIGISMUND WAS INSTRUMENTAL IN ENDING THE WESTERN SCHISM, WHICH HAD RESULTED IN NO LESS THAN THREE RIVAL POPES ALL CLAIMING TO BE THE LEGITIMATE LEADER OF THE CHURCH.

Below: The execution of Jan Hus for heresy was carried out despite Sigismund's agreement of safe passage to attend the Council of Constance.

THE HUSSITE WARS

THE HUSSITES WERE A religious movement following the teachings of Jan Hus, who was put to death for heresy in 1415. The Hussite movement encompassed most of Bavaria and spread to other regions despite no less than five crusades launched with the intention of suppressing it. The Hussites were sufficiently successful in war that they were able to launch raids into the territories of lords who opposed them or sent troops on the crusades.

Conflict began on a fairly small scale, with incidents of violence including the defenestration of several of the king's representatives in Prague. This grew into a series of wars, characterized by foreign interventions followed by lulls or internal conflict within Bohemia. The Hussites were divided into factions whose beliefs varied somewhat. This made the situation more complex, as an agreement acceptable to some Hussites might be rejected by a more radical faction.

The Hussites became famous for their innovative style of warfare, making use of early firearms and 'wagenburg' tactics based around the creation of a temporary fort by chaining wagons together. Deploying close to the enemy and maintaining a galling fire, the Hussites hoped to induce their enemies to attack their fortified position, counterattacking as they recoiled. Their discipline and fighting power were sufficient to win several engagements against the more conventional forces of various states.

Left: Hussite 'wagenberg' tactics provided a counter to the charges of heavily armoured cavalry. Composed mainly of commoners, Hussite armies could not hope to defeat their opponents in the conventional manner.

PERSECUTION OF THE JEWS

By the Middle Ages, most states in Europe had a Jewish population, whose status varied considerably. Massacres and forced conversions were not uncommon, yet at the same time Jewish merchants and physicians made an important contribution to society. The reasons for persecution varied over time and location: sometimes outsiders made a handy scapegoat for some misfortune, such as a famine or an outbreak of plague; on other occasions the motivation seems to have been financial, regardless of what excuse was used.

The motivations of Philip II Augustus of France seem to have been financial. In 1180, soon after assuming the throne, large numbers of Jews were imprisoned, or essentially forcibly robbed by the king's men. Accounts from the time present an incredible catalogue of wickedness as justification for this act,

Above: Deprived of everything but their clothing and a very small amount of money, Jews were ordered to leave France within one month. Sometimes those fleeing one round of persecution arrived just in time to face more in a different realm.

Above: Spain was a haven of tolerance for Jews under the Moors, but after the Reconquista they faced persecution or expulsion. Those accused of falsely converting to Christianity faced the Inquisition.

and go on to praise the king's kindness and compassion towards his subjects when, in 1181, Philip II cancelled all debts owed by Christians to Jews.

Philip is presented as the holy liberator of his people from their crippling debts. The 20 per cent he raked off for himself is mentioned in passing, but this blatant piece of industrial-scale robbery is presented as a good work sanctioned by a wise hermit. Likewise, contemporary accounts praise Philip's wisdom and mercy when, in 1182, he confiscated land from Jews and ordered them out of the kingdom. Those who converted to Christianity were, of course, permitted to stay.

Another expulsion, accompanied by the cancellation of debts, was carried out by Duke John of Brittany in 1240. Two years later,

King Louis IX of France – who was canonized by his own Church – ordered the burning of Jewish religious texts. Around 12,000 books – each of them painstakingly handwritten in the era before the printing press – were destroyed. Afterwards, Louis expelled Jews from his kingdom, confiscating their lands and property.

The pattern was repeated in England a few years later, conducted this time under the guise of protecting the currency. Coin clipping, the practice of shaving a little precious metal off a coin, threatened confidence in the value of currency. Severe punishments were meted out to coin clippers, but this did little to discourage the practice. Under the pretence of acting against the coin clippers, King Edward I of England arrested all the Jews in England.

Edward was already imposing heavy taxes on Jewish moneylenders to raise funds for his wars; those who could not pay the taxes were considered to be traitors who failed to support their king. Many of those arrested ostensibly for coin clipping or non-payment of taxes were executed. The lucky ones were released to find that their homes had been searched for valuables while they were imprisoned.

Special taxes and tolls were imposed upon Jews, and finally, in 1290, Edward I ordered the expulsion of all Jews from England. Naturally, limits were imposed on what they could take with them, and land and property left behind would be claimed by the crown. For the next three centuries there was virtually no Jewish presence in England.

POLAND WAS AN EXCEPTION TO THE NORM. UNDER CASIMIR III, JEWS WERE ASSURED OF THEIR PROTECTION UNDER LAW.

In the meantime, Jews had returned to France, and after 1290 were joined by some of those expelled from England. Some found a niche as royal tax collectors; others made a living however they could. This was complicated by Church rules by which Jews were forbidden to work in most fields and had to wear clothing that distinguished them. In 1306, King Philip IV ordered the arrest of all Jews in his kingdom, taking advantage of a holy day to ensure all his targets could be located at once.

Around 100,000 Jews were arrested, dispossessed of everything but the clothes they wore, and ordered to leave the country within a month. The confiscated property was auctioned off, which took years, and bounties were offered to anyone finding hidden Jewish treasure. The expulsion was cancelled in 1315, but repeated in 1322 and again on other occasions.

Those states displaying a more tolerant attitude became home for many displaced Jews. Poland, in particular, had a large Jewish community and benefited from an influx of industrious and educated people fleeing persecution elsewhere. Casimir III of Poland (1310–1370) confirmed the protections conferred by his predecessors on Jewish residents in Poland, with the effect that his state became one of the few relatively safe places in Europe.

The Moorish kingdoms of Iberia were another haven for Jews. However, after the Reconquista by the altogether less tolerant Christian states, Jews were persecuted in Spain as well. In the late 1400s, crypto-Jews (those who practised Judaism after pretending to convert to Christianity) faced the Inquisition, and in 1492 Jews were expelled from Spain. Meanwhile, the Black Death was blamed on Jews in many areas, leading to expulsions and massacres in several European states.

Above: A variety of inventive tortures were used by the Inquisition to extract confessions from crypto-Jews. Guidelines on how to spot covert Judaism were issued to the townsfolk, who were encouraged to report their suspicions to the authorities.

PHILIP IV OF FRANCE (1268–1314)

Persecutor of the Knights Templar

Louis IX of France took part in two crusades. During his second, he died in Tunisia from disease, in 1270. His son Philip, who was accompanying him, returned to take the throne of France as Philip III. Philip was known as 'the Bold' as he was a skilled and

THE WESTERN SCHISM

Above: The council of Constance ran from 1414–1418. It was primarily aimed at resolving the Western Schism, but also examined the teachings of John Wycliffe and Jan Hus. The latter was executed for heresy.

POPE URBAN VI BEGAN to offend his subordinates soon after his election in 1378, a situation that escalated until some of the cardinals declared his election void and installed a new Pope more to their liking. With Urban VI in Rome and Clement VII in Avignon, both claiming absolute authority, the Church was divided; states typically aligned themselves with whichever Pope best suited their agenda and denounced the other as Antipope. The emergence of Pope Alexander V in 1409 did nothing to simplify the situation.

The question of which Pope was legitimate could be solved only by a council that the Pope had sole authority to call. Sigismund of Hungary cut through this difficult problem by calling the Council of Constance, at which all three Popes agreed to stand down and permit the election of a new Pope who would be agreed upon by all. This was far from a simple matter, but in 1417 the Western Schism was essentially brought to an end with the installation of Martin V as Pope.

Above: Philip IV of France secured his position at the expense of popularity, and created an efficient bureaucratic apparatus to run the country. In his reign the Papal court moved to Avignon where it was under French control.

Opposite: Hoping for lasting peace with England, Philip arranged for his daughter Isabella of France to marry Edward, Prince of Wales – the future Edward II of England. Isabella was regent of England from 1326–1330 after Edward II was deposed.

aggressive warrior. Philip III reigned until 1285, like his father dying from disease contracted while on crusade. This was the Aragonese Crusade, against King Peter III of Aragon who had angered the Pope by conquering Sicily.

Philip IV succeeded his father in 1285. He was known as 'the Fair' for his good looks rather than any great interest in justice, although he tried hard to live up to the example of his grandfather, Louis IX. In fact, Philip may have tried too hard, as some of the standards he tried to attain were the exaggerated reputation of a man acclaimed as a saint.

Philip pulled out of the Aragonese Crusade upon his father's death. His early reign was spent strengthening the monarchy at the expense of the nobility, church and middle classes. This did not make him popular in any quarter, although it helped secure his position. War with England was resolved in 1303 with a dynastic marriage between Philip's daughter and the future Edward II of England. Despite a severe setback at the Battle of the Golden Spurs at Courtrai in 1302, Philip eventually defeated the Flemish, who had sided with England in the recent conflict.

Philip was also at odds with Pope Boniface VIII (1235–1303), who had challenged some of his decrees. A period of accusation and counteraccusation continued long after the death of Boniface, leading eventually to Pope Clement V moving the Papacy from Rome to Avignon, where it remained from 1309 to 1376. During the Western Schism, Avignon was again the home of a Pope, although supporters of the other candidates would refer to the Avignon rival as an Antipope.

His wars left Philip IV with a depleted treasury, a problem he tried to solve in 1306 by expelling Jews from his realm and seizing their possessions. He also targeted the Knights Templar.

pres ce que le Roy phelipe qui
fu filz mons Saint loys fu mort
Regna en france le Roy phelipe son
filz ain sn cap · le phelipe le bel · sint · hnit

The Templars were originally founded as a crusading order
whose mission was to protect the poor and the pious on their
way to the Holy Land. From small beginnings in the early 1200s,
the Templars grew into a large and powerful order that had been

granted lands in several states. Most importantly, the Templars were able to ensure the safe transfer of finances to and from the Holy Land, and later to other destinations.

By the early 1300s, the Knights Templar had become a financial institution, and many great nobles were in debt to them. Their power in the Holy Land had grown enormously, and there were many who resented the Templars' power and influence. Around 1304, allegations began to emerge of corruption within the order. These included charges of blasphemy, sodomy and heresy.

It suited Philip IV's purposes to persecute the Templars, and he hurled additional allegations at them of secret ceremonies where they showed contempt for the Cross. He had said similar things about Pope Boniface during their dispute, and the allegations are now generally regarded as being pure invention. At the time, however, there was sufficient outrage against the Templars that Philip was able to justify arresting them all.

PHILIP IV DEALT WITH HIS LACK OF FUNDS BY PERSECUTING THOSE WITH MONEY — FIRST JEWS, THEN THE KNIGHTS TEMPLAR.

The property of the Templars was largely transferred to the Knights of St John (also known as the Knights Hospitaller), who went on to have a long and illustrious career. The Templars, on the other hand, were destroyed. Many were tortured to obtain confessions and imprisoned; others were executed. This all suited Philip's plans; at a stroke he had eliminated a powerful group to which he owed money, and gained some of their possessions as well.

Much has been made of the fate of the Templars, with claims that they became part of a secret conspiracy to rule the world, fled to Scotland with their treasure, or even discovered America. The reality is comparatively mundane; they were eliminated in a cynical political gambit.

Philip IV was clearly something of an opportunist. He engaged in diplomatic exchanges with the distant Mongols, discussing the possibility of an alliance against Islamic forces in the Holy Land. This did not amount to anything, although in 1313 Philip announced his intention to take part in the latest crusade being formed. He died a year later, his ambition unfulfilled.

Opposite: Many Templars were put to death after lurid descriptions of their supposed heresy and denial of the Church came to light. Confessions extracted under torture 'proved' the allegations, and the order was dissolved.

3

QUEENS

Prominent female rulers – indeed, female rulers in general – were far less common than males in the Middle Ages. There are several possible reasons for this, and probably no single cause. It may be that the need to lead an army in the field and fight hand-to-hand against all comers made leadership a male preserve for purely physical reasons. It may also have been a recognition of the risks inherent in pregnancy and the inability of a heavily pregnant ruler to don armour and fight.

THERE IS also the possibility of habitual or deliberate sexism. Perhaps the idea that the characteristics required in a ruler were unladylike and might therefore deter potential suitors was a factor. It is equally possible that those who made the rules governing succession considered that women were temperamentally unsuitable to rule or lacked the mental capacity to grasp the necessary concepts.

Few of these reasons stand up to objective analysis, although there may be some credibility to the idea that a ruler had to be a

Opposite: The marriage of Isabella of Castile and Ferdinand of Aragon brought together two major states. It created an effective partnership of co-rulers who paved the way for the unification of Spain.

THE TRADITIONAL FRANKISH SYSTEM OF SUCCESSION EXCLUDED FEMALES UNLESS NO SUITABLE MALE RELATIVE COULD BE FOUND.

warrior and men are, on average, bigger and stronger than women. It may be that those who decided who was to succeed to the throne were men, and felt that rulership should be a boys-only club for reasons of their own. For all that, prominent female rulers did emerge in the medieval period despite rules that often required a distant male relative to be chosen over a close female one.

It is not really appropriate to say that these queens of the medieval world ruled as well as any man might have. They ruled, and their judge is history. Gender is irrelevant in the face of outcomes, and these queens achieved much in their reigns.

EMPRESS MATILDA (1102–1167)
Rightful Queen of England, usurped by her cousin

William the Conqueror had four sons, three of whom outlived him. To William Rufus went the throne of England; to Robert Curthose – his eldest son – William left his duchy in Normandy. The youngest of his sons, Henry, did not receive a title, but was provided for financially. Upon the death of William Rufus on a hunting expedition, Henry assumed the throne of England.

Below: Robert Curthose' attempt to take the throne of England by force from his brother Henry I came to an end with defeat at Tinchebray in 1106. The battle came about as a result of Robert's attempt to relieve the besieged castle at Tinchebray.

The circumstances surrounding William Rufus' death suggested the possibility of foul play, but Henry was not an unpopular choice as king. He had been born in England, unlike his older brother, and William Rufus had not endeared himself to the people of England. Henry's promises of reforms and subsequent marriage to Edith, daughter of the Scottish king and a member of the Saxon nobility, won him additional support among his people.

Henry I faced a challenge from his brother Robert Curthose, who considered England to be his inheritance by right of being first-born. His claim was supported by some of the Norman barons in England, but the brothers came to an agreement whereby each withdrew his claims to the other's realm. Henry felt the need to punish the barons who had risen against him, however, resulting in the rebellion of Robert of Bellême. Defeated, Robert fled to Normandy, where Henry pursued him. At the resulting Battle of Tinchebray in 1106, Henry defeated Robert and imprisoned him, making Henry I of England also the master of Normandy.

Henry produced a large number of illegitimate children, but had only two with his wife; there may have been a third who did not survive to adulthood. William, Henry's intended heir, died while trying to save his half-sister from a sinking ship in the English Channel. He then named his legitimate daughter Matilda as his heir.

Below: Empress Matilda gained her title from her first marriage, to Henry, Holy Roman Emperor. It is likely that she gained the habit of extreme arrogance at the same time. She did not endear herself to her subjects.

Matilda was originally named Adelaide, but her name was changed upon her marriage to Henry V, Holy Roman Emperor, in 1114. Crowned Empress of Germany at the same time, Matilda was 20 years younger than her husband and would outlive him. They had no children. It may have been a result of her high status that Matilda acquired an arrogant and haughty personality. Such traits were desirable in a ruler, up to a point, but Matilda was difficult to get along with.

Returning to England after her husband's death, she quarrelled fiercely with her father, notably over his insistence that she marry Geoffrey, Count of Anjou. The two hated one another, but, under orders from Henry I, they managed to produce a son who would become Henry II of England.

Henry I died in 1135, with the succession of Matilda apparently assured by oaths from his barons. However, Matilda was in France at the time her father died, creating an opportunity for Henry's nephew Stephen to seize the throne. Stephen was the son of Count Stephen of Blois and Adela, daughter of William the Conqueror. His claim was supported by many of the Anglo-Norman barons, apparently because many of them preferred to be ruled by a man. King David of Scotland did not agree and supported Matilda's claim to the throne.

At this time, the rules of primogeniture that would later be accepted were not uniform. It was common for a ruler to name his first-born as heir, but by no means certain. Often ancestral lands were given to the first-born with other territories distributed among other children. Hence William the Conqueror's eldest son received his duchy in Normandy rather than the English crown. This meant that succession was not always clear-cut, and may have contributed to the willingness of many barons to displace Matilda in favour of Stephen.

Be that as it may, Matilda was pregnant at the time and could not respond with prompt military action. King David's incursions from Scotland were defeated, but raiding continued and King Stephen was unable to cement his control over the country. This was in part because he was easily led by his barons – perhaps another reason why they favoured him over the self-assured and rather

arrogant Matilda. With a weak king and contested succession, England was gripped by what became known as the Anarchy.

In 1139, Matilda landed in England, where she was supported by her half-brother Robert, Earl of Gloucester. Robert was one – probably the first – of Henry I's many illegitimate children and proved both an able and a loyal supporter. Drawing King Stephen into battle against bad odds by threatening Lincoln Castle, Robert of Gloucester captured the king after a hard fight in which Stephen proved he was brave in battle even if he was not much of a commander or a ruler.

> KING STEPHEN WAS EASILY CONTROLLED BY THE BARONS, MAKING HIM A DESIRABLE CHOICE OF RULER IN THEIR EYES.

Although she was sometimes referred to as the Lady of England, Matilda was not always popular with the people. Her rather abrasive personality almost proved her undoing when she so offended the population of London that she was forced to flee, and soon after Robert of Gloucester was captured by a force commanded by King Stephen's wife. A prisoner exchange restored the situation to what it had been before the battle at Lincoln, and the Anarchy continued.

Empress Matilda was sterner in her resolve than King Stephen, and even after the death of the loyal Robert of Gloucester in 1147 she was determined to continue the struggle. In 1148, Matilda turned over the campaign to her son Henry – the future Henry II – and returned to France. In 1153, Henry and Stephen concluded a treaty whereby Stephen would remain king for the rest of his life, after which Henry would assume the throne. The death of Stephen the following year saw Henry crowned as the first of the Plantagenet dynasty.

Once Henry II was secure in his position, Empress Matilda retired to her estates in Normandy, dying in 1167. She had always been pious, and was an important patron of the Cistercian order towards the end of her life. Her refusal to accept the situation when she was deposed in favour of Stephen resulted in miserable years of civil war, but may have saved the country from worse. Stephen's rule was savagely criticized in the *Anglo-Saxon Chronicle* (a collection of annals recounting the history of the Anglo-Saxons). His barons did as they pleased, building castles to protect themselves against one another and against the king, using forced labour, and imprisoning wealthy people in order to steal their riches.

Under Stephen there was so much suffering among the common folk that it was said that 'Christ and his saints slept'. How much of this was due to the civil war is unclear, but it does seem that King Stephen's rule would have been almost as bad without it, and might have led to an additional period of oppression and chaos after his death. In any case, Empress Matilda was rightfully named heir to Henry I and had received oaths of fealty from her barons. It was both her right and her duty to fight for the crown and it was perhaps fortunate for the people of England that she was the eventual victor.

Above: Eleanor of Aquitaine was the most desirable marriage prospect in Europe. Attractive, educated and active, she was also the daughter of one of the most powerful noblemen on the continent, guaranteeing her husband vastly increased wealth and status.

ELEANOR OF AQUITAINE
(1122–1204)

Crusader, queen of France then of England

The duchy (and occasionally kingdom) of Aquitaine was established in the southwestern corner of France in 418. The region had been heavily Romanized in the previous centuries, and was the scene of a great deal of conflict as a result of the Völkerwanderung – the era of tribal migrations resulting from the Hunnic invasion of Europe.

From this turbulent time emerged an organized state, although it was still troubled by tribal incursions and conflict with neighbouring powers. The conquests of Clovis I, leading to the establishment of the Merovingian Empire, brought at least some of Aquitaine under Frankish control by 555, at which point it became a duchy owing allegiance to the king of Francia.

The capital of Aquitaine was established at Toulouse, which had been the capital of the Visigoth kingdom that existed in the region for a time. Under Charlemagne, Aquitaine was a kingdom directly ruled by the Carolingian king. During this period, other cities served as capitals and Toulouse was important mainly as a military base.

Above: Eleanor's first marriage was to Louis VII of France. She accompanied him on crusade, but disagreed with his plans to the point where the two became estranged. The marriage was eventually annulled on the grounds of consanguinity.

From around 850 onwards, Aquitaine was again a duchy, although it was sometimes called Guyenne and had its capital at Limoges. It was at times ruled directly by the Frankish kings and on other occasions by an appointed duke. By the birth of Eleanor of Aquitaine, around 1122, the duchy already had a long history as a major player in French politics. Eleanor's father, Duke William X, was wealthy and powerful, and as his heir the young Eleanor was a most desirable marriage prospect.

Upon her father's death, the king of France became the 15-year-old Eleanor's guardian. Not surprisingly, she was almost immediately informed that she was to wed his son Louis. The wedding took place in 1137, and soon afterwards Louis became king of France upon his father's death. The two were young and inexperienced, and they made mistakes. The result was a struggle for control of the country against powerful nobles, and along the way troops loyal to Louis perpetrated a massacre of non-combatants who had taken refuge in a church at Vitry.

Seeking to salve his own conscience and avoid the displeasure of the Pope, Louis agreed to take part in a crusade to the Holy Land. Eleanor seems to have been a strong proponent of what was to become the Second Crusade, enthusiastically offering large numbers of fighting men to the cause and speaking out in its support. Less well received was her insistence that she and some of her ladies were to accompany the army.

Eleanor had always been an active individual, and was renowned as a horsewoman in her youth. At least some of her female entourage were armoured and armed as knights, though there is no indication they entered battle. During the crusade, Eleanor and Louis became increasingly estranged. Louis was dead set on reaching Jerusalem, but Eleanor sided with her uncle, Raymond of Poitiers. In this she may have shown better strategic vision than her husband.

Raymond of Poitiers wanted to secure Edessa, which had been the capital of the Crusader County of Edessa until its fall in 1144. Indeed, the loss of Edessa was the primary reason for launching a crusade; along with its spiritual and political significance, the city would be an important base for the consolidation of Crusader power in the Holy Land. Eleanor may have perceived this better than her husband or may have been swayed by the arguments of her uncle. They certainly spent a lot of time together, prompting rumours of a liaison that were almost certainly false.

Louis' demand that Eleanor support his bid for Jerusalem provoked great resentment. She declared their marriage invalid on grounds of consanguinity – they were too closely related – but still accompanied the advance on Jerusalem. Ultimately, the crusade failed to capture Jerusalem and the two returned home

Above: Eleanor insisted on taking with her a large entourage on crusade. This was not unusual in itself, but some aspects, such as equipping ladies as knights, attracted disapproval.

separately. Although they remained married for a time and had two daughters, Eleanor and Louis were never reconciled. In 1152, the marriage of Eleanor and Louis was annulled on the grounds of consanguinity.

After successfully resisting the attempts of several powerful noblemen to arrange marriages that suited their plans, Eleanor married Henry of Anjou – the future Henry II of England – in 1152. Henry became king of England in 1154, and was so powerful that his holdings are often referred to as the Angevin Empire. With the addition of Aquitaine by marriage, Henry's reign marked the greatest extent of English power in France, and Eleanor was highly active in its rule. Over the next two decades she bore her husband eight children, but in 1173 she was imprisoned after being implicated in a plot by two of her sons against the king.

ALTHOUGH THE ROBIN HOOD STORY PORTRAYS JOHN AS THE UNPOPULAR REGENT, IT WAS IN FACT ELEANOR OF AQUITAINE WHO RULED IN HER SON RICHARD'S STEAD.

Upon the death of Henry II, he was succeeded his son, Richard. Richard I (better known as the Lionheart) ordered Eleanor's release and made her regent in England while he was away on the Third Crusade. One outcome of Eleanor's insistence on taking an entourage of women to the Holy Land during the Second Crusade was a papal edict that women were henceforth banned from crusading. While Richard was away, Philip II of France attacked his holdings on the continent, and Richard was imprisoned while hurrying home to deal with the problem.

Eleanor was involved in the negotiations for Richard's release, but after his death in 1199 and the succession of his brother John to the throne she played little part in the affairs of England other than as an emissary to the French throne. Eleanor returned to Aquitaine, where she remained an active and formidable woman, personally going to Castile in her late seventies to bring her granddaughter Blanche to marry the French king. After turning 80, she defended Aquitaine from an attempt by Arthur of Brittany to annex it, but retired once the duchy was safe. She died in 1204.

A crusader as well as separately the queen of both England and France, Eleanor of Aquitaine was also instrumental in

Opposite: Eleanor was instrumental in developing the concept of chivalry as we have come to know it. Here, her granddaughter Blanche of Castile listens to poetry.

n non de dieu   m ais ce me fait reconforter
le creatour   q' me daigmerent gmander
q uour dinst   q ie ceste estoire entendisse
psa grat doucour   z a rimer lentrepreisse
oclelames li   .ij. dames enau maint la flour
puissons rendre   d e sens de biaute de valour
wrai arimouer   l eur nons ne vueil en apt dire
entendre   c ar leur pais aim z dout leur ire

s ique bien sai quele morroie

d e duel se fait ne dit auoie

J e qui fil dogier le danois   R iens fors leur plaisir z leur gre

z de bertain qui fu ou bois

z de buenon de conmarchis

CHIVALRY

THE CONCEPT OF CHIVALRY evolved throughout the Middle Ages, with the armoured knight changing – in theory at least – from a professional cavalryman to a paragon of virtue who was also skilled at fighting. Various versions of the 'code of chivalry' existed, placing greater or lesser emphasis on religion and protection of the Church. There was a general agreement that honesty, generosity and courage were virtues to aspire to, but the degree to which the code was followed could vary considerably.

Other institutions also evolved. Originally, a tourney was nothing more than a meeting of knights who tested their skills against one another – often with live weapons – and could take place almost anywhere. Later, tourneys were grand events filled with pageantry and politics, at which an ambitious knight could win a fortune or establish a fearsome reputation. The evolution of the social aspects of knighthood occurred alongside technological developments that ultimately led to the creation of specialist tournament armour unsuited to the battlefield – arguably the world's most expensive sporting equipment.

Left: The joust developed from an almost casual encounter or contest into a formal event accompanied by feasting and pageantry. As armour improved it became a little less dangerous, but fatalities still occurred and injuries were common.

the development of what would become known as chivalry. Originally the term referred to being in possession of a horse, which was the basic indicator of wealth and status. Well-off fighting men, even those dubbed as knights, were typically still rough men of war without much in the way of social graces. Ironically, perhaps, Eleanor was influenced by the cultured ways of the Moors, who at the time dominated Spain, and preferred her knights to behave with some semblance of civility.

Eleanor implemented many aspects of what is sometimes known as 'courtly love', with knights encouraged to behave with elaborate courtesy and to compose poems praising Eleanor and her ladies. Those who wanted the favour of the court or the favours of a lady had to play the game. This encouraged the spread of education among the warrior class and the idea of the 'gentle knight' that dominated the later medieval era.

BLANCHE OF CASTILE (1188–1252)

Twice regent of France

Eleanor of Aquitaine had 10 children, two by King Louis of France and eight by her second husband, Henry II of England. Most survived to adulthood and played important roles in the politics of the time as consorts, dukes, earls and even kings. Among them was Eleanor of England, Eleanor's second daughter with Henry II. Eleanor of England was born in 1162 and at the age of 12 married King Alfonso VIII of Castile.

Alliance with Spanish kings was important to the security of Aquitaine and, by association, other English holdings in France. If Aquitaine were threatened then forces might be drawn away from other territories, leaving them vulnerable to attack by an ambitious French king. This was not entirely successful; Alfonso of Castile began to claim that Gascony was part of Eleanor's dowry and launched a campaign to take it in 1205. The claim was withdrawn after some negotiation, although the idea that Gascony had been promised to Castile would re-remerge later.

Above: Blanche of Castile was first married to Louis VIII of France, to whom she bore the future Louis IX – Saint Louis. Blanche acted as regent until Louis IX was old enough to rule in his own right.

Eleanor of England secured good marriages for her daughters, and became so powerful in Castile that she was to all intents and purposes a co-ruler rather than a consort. She died in 1214 just weeks after her husband, apparently consumed with grief. In the meantime, her eldest daughters married the kings of Leon and Aragon, and her third daughter, Blanche, was wed to the king of France.

Blanche of Castile was escorted to France by her formidable grandmother, Eleanor of Aquitaine, who was almost 80 years old. The wedding took place in 1200, but was not consummated immediately. Blanche was at the time 12 years old, and her husband Louis was 13. The marriage was arranged by King John of England, who was in the process of losing most of his father Henry II's huge territory in France and desperately needed peace.

Below: The marriage of Blanche and Louis was arranged by King John of England, who hoped to create peace between England and France. This gave Louis a tenuous claim to the throne of England, legitimizing intervention in John's civil war against his barons.

Although she was of the English and Castilian royal lines, Blanche was loyal to her adopted homeland and pressed for the unification of France. This would inevitably be at the cost of England, but since John Lackland, as he was nicknamed, had already lost most of his holdings there, little significant conflict of interest existed.

In 1215, King John of England was forced to agree the Magna Carta with his barons, but his failure to abide by its provisions quickly resulted in civil war. Seeking support against the king of England, the barons invited Louis of France to intervene. He did so, citing his wife Blanche's claim to the English throne as a granddaughter of Henry II. King John died and his son became Henry III at a time when Louis of France held London and much of the south and Blanche was raising funds and troops on the continent. After more fighting, Louis made peace with England and returned home. He was crowned king of France in 1223, though he reigned for only three years.

Much of Blanche's career was against the backdrop of the Cathari heresy. The Cathars rejected much of the Old Testament and favoured a rather extreme form of religion based on asceticism and renunciation of the material world. Their teachings directly opposed mainstream Catholicism in many places and became a serious concern as they spread.

In 1208, Pope Innocent III called for a crusade against the heretics. This became known as the Albigensian Crusade for Albi, a French city where the movement had a great deal of support. The counts of Toulouse were tolerant towards the Cathari sect and had hopes of becoming independent from the French crown. The crusade was popular for many reasons, including the fact that crusaders could gain all the religious benefits of being on

AT THE TIME OF KING JOHN'S DEATH, LOUIS WAS IN CONTROL OF LONDON AND BLANCHE WAS RAISING ADDITIONAL FUNDS TO SUPPORT HIM.

Below: After initially trying to curb Catharism by sending missionaries to preach mainstream Catholicism, Pope Innocent III called for a crusade. The heresy was suppressed by direct and often brutal means.

crusade without having to trek all the way to the Holy Land. Indeed, each spring as the campaign season began new forces would muster, returning home in the winter with their duty done.

Regardless of the rather cynical nature of this type of crusading, the campaign against the Cathars was savage and involved indiscriminate massacres of towns thought to be harbouring heretics. The south of France was more or less pacified by 1215, but rose in rebellion once the attention of the Church was directed towards a crusade in the Middle East. Louis VIII led a successful campaign to pacify the south of France, defeating the counts of Toulouse, but died in 1226 leaving his young son to be crowned Louis IX.

Blanche of Castile was named as regent, and ruled France in her son's name until he was old enough to take up the reins of power. The French politics of the time were always vigorous, and with a boy-king on the throne there were those who sought to advance their own position. Among them was count Philip Hurepel of Boulogne, an illegitimate son of Philip II of France.

BLANCHE OF CASTILE RULED FRANCE AS REGENT WHILST HER SON WAS A CHILD, AND AGAIN FROM 1248–1252 WHILST HE WAS AWAY ON CRUSADE.

Philip Hurepel's uprising was supported by Henry III of England and had a real chance of success. Blanche of Castile raised an army and marched to meet the rebels, but was able to agree a treaty rather than fight. The agreement did not last, requiring a military campaign coupled with excellent diplomacy to pacify the country.

Among Blanche's achievements was a reconciliation with her cousin, Count Raymond of Toulouse, leading to the eventual marriage of his daughter Jeanne to Blanche's son Alphonse. Upon Raymond's death, she acted swiftly to forestall any attempt to depose Jeanne and Alphonse, extracting oaths of fidelity from their vassals before any plot could mature. In the meantime, Blanche was able to bring the rebellion against her son Louis IX to an end by negotiating from a position of strength. She also intervened in European politics on a wider scale, helping to arrange dynastic marriages and opposing others.

Opposite: The city of Toulouse was besieged and changed hands repeatedly during the Albigensian Crusade. Its ruler, Count Raymond VI, was accused of being too tolerant of the Cathars.

Above: Blanche was a protector of those who were powerless under the social system of the time, such as Jews or the very poor.

Blanche of Castile was a protector of the poor and of Jews, opposing the general sentiment of the time. In this she showed a remarkable readiness to go against the prevailing opinions of the time, even if it damaged her own popularity. Blanche did, however, fall out with the University of Paris, resulting in the withdrawal of students and academics from the facility. A settlement was eventually reached, with the university gaining additional privileges and protections.

BENEFIT OF CLERGY

In 1166, Henry II of England streamlined the legal system, which previously required a secular magistrate and a senior member of the clergy to hear legal cases. One probably unintended consequence was that a secular court had no authority over clergymen, since they had the right to have their cases heard by an ecclesiastical court.

It became the practice that anyone who could 'prove' they were a member of the clergy could have their case transferred to an ecclesiastical court, where sentences were far more lenient and might require nothing more than an act of penance. Initially, dressing and looking the part of a clergyman was accepted as proof, but later this was amended to the ability to read a passage from the Bible. Since the relevant passage was almost always the 51st Psalm, an enterprising rogue could avoid serious punishment by claiming 'benefit of clergy' and reciting the psalm from memory to prove it.

Restrictions were later added to curb this practice, and some offences were declared too serious to allow benefit of clergy. These included witchcraft, murder, treason and – curiously – pickpocketing. The amount of power a state or its king had to punish members of the Church remained a bone of contention throughout the era.

When Louis IX came of age and began to rule in his own right, Blanche of Castile continued to support him and played an important role in his administration of France. She was not, however, friendly to his wife, Margaret of Provence, even though Blanche had advocated the match in the first place. Blanche particularly disapproved of Louis' decision to go on crusade with his wife, but was an able regent in his name while he was away.

Blanche was by all accounts a genuinely pious woman, who did many good works. Some of them were inspired by an incident in which she made desperate vows to God while her children were ill, but was unsure of exactly what she had promised. Her solution was to petition the Pope to approve of a conversion of these vows to a promise to do goodly works. It is likely that much of her mercy and protection towards the poor and oppressed came from a genuinely good spirit, however.

BLANCHE OF CASTILE RESOLVED HER DISPUTE WITH THE UNIVERSITY OF PARIS BY AWARDING ADDITIONAL PRIVILEGES TO STUDENTS OF THE INSTITUTION.

During Blanche's regency and the reign of her son Louis IX, the Church benefited from her patronage and from a period of general prosperity and stability. This allowed cathedrals and monasteries to be built, notably by the Cistercians, who Blanche favoured. She died of a heart condition in 1252 and was buried at Maubuisson Abbey, of which she was the patron.

ISABELLA OF FRANCE (1292–1358)
Deposed her husband, regent for her son
Isabella of France was the daughter of Philip IV of France and Joan of Navarre. She was born at a time when England and France were intermittently in conflict, before the beginning of the Hundred Years' War. Up until this point it was still possible for English nobles or even a king to ask for assistance from France; within a few years this would become unthinkable.

Above: Wisely seeking to cement peace with England, Philip IV secured a marriage between his daughter Isabella and the future Edward II. It was not a happy union, ending in armed conflict between Isabella and Edward.

Isabella's father was elevated to heir upon the death of his older brother, which was sudden and accompanied by rumours and accusations. His own father was distant, having been devastated by the loss of his first wife. Philip found a role model in Louis IX, who was canonized, and he tried to live up to what he imagined Louis' standards to be.

In 1294, war with England broke out over ownership of Gascony, with a young and not very confident Philip opposed by Edward I of England. Matters went better than might have been expected, and in 1303 a treaty was concluded that promised a marriage between the future Edward II of England and Isabella, Philip's daughter.

Edward I died while on campaign against the Scots in 1307, placing his son Edward II on the throne of England. The promised marriage to Isabella took place the following year. Almost immediately, Isabella became embroiled in the complex politics of England, notably the controversy surrounding the king's favourite, Piers Gaveston. Much has been written about the relationship between Piers and Edward, with allegations that they were lovers. It is equally possible that they were simply close friends, brothers by choice rather than birth.

Be that as it may, Gaveston was repeatedly exiled to reduce his influence over the king, once on the orders of Edward I and twice as a result of pressure from English barons and the French crown. Isabella herself lamented that Piers Gaveston had taken her place in the king's life, but this does not necessarily stand as proof of a sexual relationship. She may instead have been commenting on the fact that as the king's wife she would expect to be his confidante and deputy – roles that Piers Gaveston had usurped. The enmity of the English nobility, voiced through

PIERS GAVESTON WON HIMSELF A PLACE IN THE ROYAL HOUSEHOLD, BUT ONCE THERE THE HONOURS LAVISHED UPON HIM BY EDWARD CAUSED SEVERE RESENTMENT.

Below: Whilst the relationship between Edward II and Piers Gaveston is open to debate, its nature was probably less important than the power Gaveston wielded because of it.

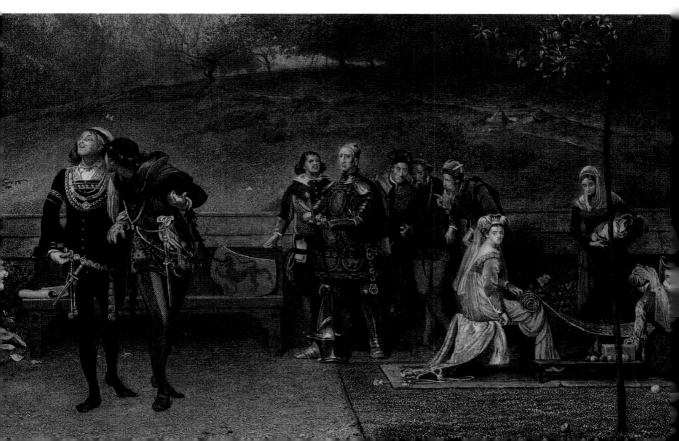

accusations that Gaveston and Edward II were lovers, may well have resulted from more pragmatic concerns about the amount of influence Gaveston wielded.

Isabella appealed to her friends at court, relatives from France and the Pope for support in her power struggle with Gaveston, and in 1311 he was exiled for the third and final time. Under pain of outlawry, he returned anyway, which made him fair game for his enemies. They took the opportunity for all it was worth and executed Gaveston. Among them was Thomas, Earl of Lancaster, who was related to Isabella and may have been sympathetic to her situation or simply acting out of self-interest.

GAVESTON'S ENEMIES PRODUCED AN ORDINANCE DEMANDING HE BE PERMANENTLY EXILED. THE KING DECLARED THIS UNLAWFUL, BRINGING ABOUT OPEN CONFLICT.

Possibly as a result of the Gaveston problem, relations between Isabella and her husband became increasingly strained, although she bore him children. Edward's prestige was badly dented by defeat at Bannockburn in 1314, and he had a new set of favourites, the Despenser family. Escalating tensions between the Despensers and other English lords, notably the Earl of Lancaster, resulted in civil war that ended with a royal – it might be better to say Despenser – victory and the execution of Lancaster.

Secure in their position, the Despensers took every opportunity to enrich themselves, although they made sure Edward II benefited too. By the early 1320s, popular opinion had hardened against Edward and his favourites; oft-repeated tales began to turn Lancaster into a martyr. Meanwhile, Roger Mortimer, one of the leading opponents of the Despensers, escaped from his imprisonment in the Tower of London in 1323 and fled to France.

Two years later, Isabella also journeyed to France, ostensibly to settle the dispute over Gascony that had recently flared up into conflict. She declined to return to England, claiming (perhaps with some justification) that the Despensers meant her harm. Isabella began plotting against her estranged husband with the assistance of Roger Mortimer. The two became lovers at some point, although it is unclear when. It is possible that they were involved before they left England, but it was not until 1326 that their relationship was acknowledged.

Isabella had been joined in France by her son, the future Edward III, making her refusal to come home more damaging to Edward II. He expected an invasion and made what preparations he could, but the excesses of the Despensers resulted in a lack of enthusiasm among the rest of the nobility for the royal cause. Support for Isabella's expedition was rather greater, and the ranks of her force swelled rapidly as opponents of the Despensers came over to her side. Edward II and his supporters fled London, leaving behind numerous officials to become victims of the angry citizens.

Edward II and the Despensers tried to rally support, but found little, and were rapidly defeated. Edward was imprisoned for a time while his supporters were harshly dealt with, and proceedings began to replace Edward II with his teenage son. With no precedent to work from, it was necessary to make an appeal to the nobility and clergy of England, to the effect that Edward II's rule had been bad for everyone other than his favourites, and he had thus demonstrated that he was unfit to

Opposite: Gaveston was captured after being besieged at Scarborough Castle. His enemies were more interested in getting rid of him than with the niceties of law, and quickly had him executed after a pretence of a trial.

Above: The young Edward III was crowned king of England upon the abdication of his father. During the subsequent regency, Roger Mortimer made enemies by excessive favouritism.

EDWARD, THE BLACK PRINCE (1330–1376)

EDWARD WAS THE SON of Edward III of England, and was trained to war from an early age. Although he was only 16 at the time of the Battle of Crécy in 1346, his father sufficiently trusted Edward's prowess to 'let him win his spurs' rather than coming to the assistance of the prince's hard-pressed force. At Poitiers in 1356 he defeated a larger force commanded by King John of France and captured the French king.

Edward was renowned as a chivalrous knight, although the nickname the Black Prince – given long after his death – may have resulted from his temper, which

Left: Edward III was succeeded by Richard II, his grandson, due to the untimely death of Edward, the Black Prince.

was not always held in check. He loved luxury and ostentation, and among the noble guests at his court in Aquitaine were kings-in-exile. One such was Peter of Castile, who asked Edward to assist in regaining his throne. Edward became ill during this campaign and never recovered, dying in 1376 at the age of 46. His father Edward III did not die until the following year, passing the throne to Richard, son of Edward the Black Prince.

rule. The country agreed, but there was a question of succession – the young Edward's claim to the throne came by way of his father, and might be invalidated by his removal from the throne. Instead, Edward II was forced to abdicate in favour of his son.

Edward III was 14 years old when he was crowned in 1327, and for a time England was governed by Isabella and Mortimer. However, Mortimer began to behave as his enemies had, consolidating his power and ensuring that his supporters prospered even at the expense of others. A plot to remove him failed, largely because Edward III did not support it, but in 1330 Edward had Mortimer and Isabella arrested. Mortimer was put to death; Isabella was treated more leniently.

**Above: Edward III had
planned to move against
Mortimer for some time,
but it was not until
October 1330 that he was
able to do so. Around
20 trusted knights took
part in the arrest at
Nottingham Castle.**

After a period of arrest, Isabella was granted an income from
the crown and permitted to live as an English noblewoman
should, although she forfeited most of her holdings. Isabella was
active at court during the rest of her life, and also made religious
pilgrimages. As was not uncommon at the time, she entered a
holy order before her death.

As well as being instrumental in the overthrow of Edward II,
Isabella was influential in the life of her grandson – Edward, the
Black Prince – to whom she left most of her remaining property
upon her death in 1358.

THE STABILITY OF THE KINGDOM
OF NAPLES WAS THREATENED
BY POWER STRUGGLES AFTER
THE YOUNG JOANNA CAME TO
THE THRONE.

JOANNA I OF NAPLES (1328–1382)

Lost and regained control of her own realm

The kingdom of Naples originated in the
early twelfth century as a result of Norman
conquests in Sicily and southern Italy. It
became a separate political entity towards the

end of the century, with Sicily passing under Aragonese control. In the early to mid-1300s, Naples was ruled by King Robert the Wise, and enjoyed stability and prosperity.

King Robert was renowned as a patron of the arts and an advocate of education, and spent considerable sums on the construction of imposing buildings. Under his rule, Naples grew into a centre for learning and progressive thought. Robert's sons died while he was still on the throne, creating a problem with succession. He chose the eldest of his grandchildren, Joanna, who was already betrothed. King Robert was adamant that Joanna would be ruler in her own right. Her husband would receive titles appropriate to his station, but Robert would pass his legacy to his granddaughter.

Joanna was a member of the Capetian Angevin dynasty, a cadet branch of the house of Capet that ruled France from the late tenth century the early fourteenth until. This meant that she had powerful relatives all over Europe who might be able to lend support, but also that she could be drawn into their own troubles. In addition to the Kingdom of Naples, Joanna inherited the titles of Countess of Provence and of Forcalquier.

As Joanna was only 16 years old when her grandfather died, a regency was implemented. Naturally, power struggles developed around the throne, with the regency being taken over by a papal legate. The following year, 1344, Joanna

Below: Under the rule of Robert the Wise, culture and learning flowered in the Kingdom of Naples. Years of prosperity enabled grand buildings to be constructed.

Above: Joanna of Naples tried both involving and keeping her husbands out of the affairs of state. Neither approach ended very well.

Opposite: The murder of Andrew of Hungary was carried out in a particularly brutal manner and resulted in a breakdown of relations with his home nation. Joanna was declared innocent of any part in the incident.

was crowned Queen of Naples. Her husband, Andrew of Hungary, was honoured, but given no official position, about which he protested vigorously.

Andrew took advantage of Joanna's illness to advance his own plans, resulting in him becoming unpopular among other members of the nobility. He also secured a deal with the Pope to have himself crowned king of Naples and to take an active role in its governance. He was murdered in 1345 while on a hunting trip – he was strangled with a cord and thrown out of the window in the middle of the night. Joanna was nearby, but opinions remain divided as to whether she was involved in the plot. She was pregnant at the time with their child, who was born at the end of the year. The murder of Andrew soured relations with Hungary, which were already strained by the decision not to involve him in the government of 'his' new realm. There was an expectation that Joanna would marry Andrew's younger brother Stephen, so the announcement of Joanna's forthcoming marriage to Louis of Taranto was not well received.

Naples was already under threat, having lost most of its holdings in Piedmont to attacks from northern Italy, and the marriage to Louis of Taranto caused additional enemies to appear. These included Robert of Taranto – Louis' brother – and Charles of Durazzo. Although Louis and Joanna were successful against Robert's forces, the Hungarians also invaded Naples in 1347.

With no hope of resisting the invasion with the resources of their realm, Louis and Joanna fled the city of Naples ahead of the advancing Hungarians. The couple went to Provence by way of Marseille and thence journeyed to Avignon for an audience with the Pope, who blessed their marriage and agreed to investigate the murder of Joanna's first husband, Andrew. Eventually Joanna was pronounced innocent of any complicity. In the meantime, an outbreak of the Black Death caused the Hungarians to withdraw from Naples, creating an opportunity to return. Joanna did so, beginning a joint reign with her new husband Louis, in contrast to her earlier treatment of Andrew as a mere consort.

War with Hungary continued for some time, and Louis'

role as military commander in a time of crisis allowed him to gradually assume control of Naples. He replaced Joanna's favoured and trusted officials with his own, possibly executing those he particularly disliked. He died in 1362, having outlived all of Joanna's children.

With Louis dead, Joanna set about restoring her control over her kingdom, removing officials who were not to her liking and passing new laws to consolidate her position. She married again, by proxy at the end of 1362 and in person the following year. Her new husband was James IV of Majorca, a rather troubled individual who had spent nearly 14 years imprisoned in an iron cage as a result of the power struggles around his throne.

James IV of Majorca was unstable after his long imprisonment, and obsessed with regaining his kingdom rather than helping Joanna. rule Naples.

Joanna had no surviving children, and wanted an heir more than she wanted a husband. James was excluded from the government of Naples by their marriage contract, and was a consort only. In any case, he was still intent on recovering the throne of Majorca and departed to Castile on campaign with Edward the Black Prince of England, whom he hoped might restore him to his own realm. The campaign went badly and James was captured. Joanna ransomed him, but he very soon embarked on another adventure in Castile, where he died in 1375.

James did not give Joanna an heir, although he did bequeath to her his claim to the principality of Achaea. Over the next few years, Joanna's holdings in Provence were threatened by conflict there, although this was not directed against her. Naples itself was at peace, allowing Joanna to focus on administration and lawmaking. Despite a tendency to micromanage the affairs of her state, Joanna was an effective ruler under whom prosperity increased. Her handling of internal power plays increased the strength of her position, and in 1376 she married Otto, Duke of Brunswick-Grubenhagen, who had campaigned on her behalf during the recent troubles. Otto was explicitly a prince consort; Joanna did not want to repeat earlier mistakes.

The QUEEN of NAPLES surrenders her DOMINIONS
to POPE CLEMENT 7th

Vol. V. 06.

In 1378, the Church was divided by what became known as the Western Schism, with two rival popes elected; one in Rome and one in Avignon. There was no way to stay out of such a conflict; in any case, Joanna had political ties to Avignon and thus to Pope Clement VII, who was supported by the French crown. His enemy, Urban VI, denounced Joanna and refused to recognize her rulership of Naples, ensuring that her realm was fair game for ambitious lords.

Charles of Durazzo had plenty of ambition, and had recently been unsuccessful in his bid to increase his power within Naples. With the support of forces supplied by Hungary, he invaded Naples and defeated Otto of Brunswick-Grubenhagen. Joanna was besieged and forced to surrender. During her

Above: The Western Schism did more than divide the Church; kingdoms were forced to decide where their loyalties lay. Joanna of Naples sided with Clement VII, Pope in Avignon, and thus made an enemy of Urban IV.

Above: According to some sources, Joanna was smothered to death. Others say she was strangled with a cord. Her first husband was killed in this manner, and although Joanna was pronounced innocent there were those who continued to blame her.

imprisonment, Louis I of Anjou, who the childless Joanna had named as her heir, advanced into Italy in the hope of freeing her. He was too late; Otto was exiled from Naples and Joanna had been murdered.

Some accounts claim that Joanna was strangled with a cord, in a manner not dissimilar to the way her first husband died. Others state that she was smothered with pillows or a mattress. However it happened, the official version was that she had died a natural death, and her body was placed on display as proof that she really was dead. It was then disposed of without honours since Joanna was an excommunicate – at least according to one Pope.

Joanna's death ended the era of stability previously enjoyed by Naples; disputes over succession wracked the kingdom for many years thereafter. Joanna's holdings in Provence and Forcalquier passed to Louis I of Anjou.

THE BLACK DEATH

THE BLACK DEATH WAS most likely brought to Europe from Asia by fleas living on rats aboard merchant ships, and spread rapidly through the extensive trading links that existed at the time. Caused by the *Yersinia pestis* bacterium, the Black Death could take the form of one of several diseases typically known as 'plague'. Bubonic plague was the commonest of these.

The plague had a very high mortality rate, but was not present everywhere at once – largely as a result of killing its hosts. As a result, the politics of the time were heavily influenced by which regions had been depopulated by plague, and which currently had it. The plague also caused secondary problems such as the belief that it was a punishment from God, leading to the massacre of Jews, gypsies or foreigners in some areas.

The Black Death was one of the factors that brought the Middle Ages to a close. So many people died that a day's work by an unskilled labourer became a valuable commodity, enabling ordinary people to demand better treatment and fairer wages, and ultimately dissolving the medieval social order.

Left: The Black Death inspired fear and horror throughout Europe, scarring the psyche of communities that lived through it and forever changing the social order.

Right: King Valdemar IV of Denmark holds Visby to ransom. Although a form of taxation, this sort of activity is more akin to robbery or extortion. The townsfolk were required to fill three large vessels with valuables, and if they failed Visby would be burned to the ground.

MARGARET I OF DENMARK (1353–1412)

Ruler of a unified Scandinavia

Denmark was heavily involved in the politics of England and Scotland, as well as many other nations, throughout the medieval period. One of the homelands of the Norsemen, often called Vikings, Denmark was the point of origin for trading and raiding expeditions, and later for large forces that conquered or settled new lands. The people of Denmark had much in common with those of

Sweden and Norway, with strong links via coastal trade, ensuring
that the history of the Scandinavian nations would be intertwined.

Denmark became Christianized in the mid-tenth century due to
the choices of King Harald Bluetooth, who also succeeded in making
himself king of Norway for a time. Denmark's society evolved from
an early medieval culture into a feudal kingdom of the High Middle
Ages. By the birth of Margaret in 1353, it was prone to the same
type of dynastic troubles as other European states.

Margaret's grandfather was Christopher II, who was elected king by members of the great nobility precisely because they expected him to be weak and ineffectual. He took over a realm that had been mortgaged under unfavourable terms to various Danish and German lords, and was bound by a charter that required the consent of the great nobility and the Church before the king could take any action.

With many possible sources of revenue denied to him by the charter, which heavily favoured those who had imposed it, Christopher II tried to make money from warfare against the states of northern Germany. He was deposed by the great nobility in 1326 and spent three years in exile before squabbling among the nobles resulted in an invitation to become king once more. Christopher II inherited an even worse situation than before. His subsequent reign, if that is the right term, was as a puppet; upon his death, Denmark ceased to be a kingdom at all.

CHRISTOPHER II OF DENMARK INHERITED A MISERABLE SITUATION AND WAS UNABLE TO IMPROVE IT. UPON HIS DEATH, DENMARK CEASED TO BE A KINGDOM AT ALL.

Further internal problems in Denmark led to Margaret's father Valdemar – son of Christopher II – being recalled from exile and installed as king of Denmark. Again, the great landholders really wanted nothing more than a figurehead, but Valdemar IV had other ideas. Diplomacy gained him some territory from which to raise money – notably by taxation of shipping through the narrow seas off Copenhagen, and he came to an agreement with the Teutonic order to cede them Danish Estonia in return for cash with which he paid off the mortgages on some additional lands.

Opposite: Margaret of Denmark was used, like many royal daughters, as a political pawn by her father Valdemar IV. Married to king Haakon of Norway, she was to cement an alliance that would improve the standing of Valdemar's re-emerging kingdom.

By a combination of diplomacy and force, Valdemar IV made himself king of a renewed Denmark. The outbreak of the bubonic plague in 1349 hit Valdemar's enemies harder than his supporters, enabling him to annex yet more land. His later reign was characterized by conflict with Sweden and with the Hanseatic League, whose growing power was more than he could challenge. Valdemar IV died in 1375, having rebuilt the kingdom of Denmark out of virtually nothing.

Valdemar was succeeded by his daughter Margaret, who was married to King Haakon of Norway. The match had been arranged by her father when she was very young as a means to strengthen the Danish position and, despite some turbulent politics, the two were married in 1363. Haakon had hoped to

also gain the throne of Sweden, but his military campaign was defeated by Albert of Mecklenburg, who was crowned king of Sweden in 1364.

Margaret was educated in Norway, and when her father died in 1375 her young son Olaf was elected king of Denmark. The death of Haakon in 1380 made Olaf king of Norway as well, and Margaret ruled both as regent. In this she was highly successful; indeed, she is credited with essentially ruling Norway even before the death of King Haakon. The union between Denmark and Norway that began with Margaret and Olaf lasted long after the end of the medieval era. In the meantime, Margaret was able to successfully challenge the Hanseatic League for control of some coastal territories previously lost to them.

After Olaf came of age, Margaret began preparations for a campaign into Sweden in his name. Her intent was to depose Albert of Mecklenburg and make Olaf king of Sweden as well. Olaf's death in 1387 derailed this plan and threatened Margaret's position as de facto queen of Norway and Denmark. However, adroit diplomacy enabled Margaret not only to retain her position but to strengthen it, and her nephew Erik of Pomerania was named heir to the joint realm.

Meanwhile, Albert of Mecklenburg had alienated many of his nobles and was facing rebellion. Seizing on a dispute over the will of Bo Jonsson Grip, the highest official in Sweden, Margaret entered the conflict and was well received by the Swedish nobles who proclaimed her their rightful ruler. Albert of Mecklenburg was made a prisoner until the last of his supporters had been pacified.

Margaret had succeeded in doing what many Scandinavian monarchs had aspired to: she had unified Denmark, Norway and Sweden under a single ruler. Erik of Pomerania was declared king of Norway, with succession on a hereditary basis, in 1389, and in 1396 Denmark and Sweden elected him their king. This also gave him control over Finland, which had been a territory of Bo Jonsson Grip.

MARGARET OF DENMARK CREATED A UNIFIED SCANDINAVIA, AND WAS DE FACTO RULER EVEN AFTER ERIK OF POMERANIA HAD BEEN FORMALLY CROWNED.

Opposite: Erik of Pomerania was a grandson of Valdemar IV of Denmark, and was also related to Haakon of Norway. With a claim to both realms his selection also legitimized Margaret's continuing stewardship.

Erik was crowned at Kalmar in Sweden, although Margaret continued to rule the united realm in fact if not in name. Her authoritarian style was not universally popular, but she was successful in reducing the power of the nobility and consolidating authority with the throne. Some of her actions, such as seizing Church lands, might have led to disaster, but were conducted from such a strong position that there was little effective opposition.

Margaret died in 1412 during a campaign to reincorporate Holstein into her realm. By then, her heir Erik was married to Philippa, daughter of Henry IV of England, and the future of her unified Scandinavia seemed secure. In the event, at least part of the union – that between Norway and Denmark – would last until 1814.

ISABELLA I OF CASTILE (1441–1504)

Reformer, Co-leader of the Reconquista

The Iberian peninsula was conquered by the Umayyad Caliphate in the eighth century, with further expansion into Europe vigorously opposed by the Franks. During the years of conflict that followed, some areas of the peninsula were reconquered, creating Christian states that were not always at odds with their Islamic neighbours.

The kingdom of Castile in northern Iberia was originally part of the kingdom of Leon, and, after a period of independence, the two merged in 1230 to create the crown of Castile. Meanwhile, the neighbouring kingdom of Aragon began as part of Navarre, but grew into a powerful state in its own right.

During the troubled years that followed, more of the Iberian peninsula was reconquered, and both Aragon and Castile became players on the political stage of Europe. Their fortunes, like those of any realm, were mixed, and Isabella's father John II came to the throne at only a few months old. By the time the regency ended in 1419 and John II was able to rule in his own right, his position was very weak. Among the troubles he faced was intriguing by the sons of King Ferdinand of neighbouring Aragon, who had been one of the regents during John's early reign.

John's chief ally during this period was Alvaro de Luna, his constable and favourite. Luna had no wealth of his own, and benefited greatly from his association with John, but did support him through some very difficult times. John II had four children by his first marriage, to Maria of Aragon, but only one, the future Henry IV of Castile, survived to adulthood. In 1447, he married Isabella of Portugal, and Alvaro de Luna fell sufficiently out of favour that he was executed in 1453.

John II died in 1454, by which time he had two children by Isabella of Portugal, though their second child, Alphonso, died in his teens. Henry IV succeeded to the throne of Castile, but

Below: Although each had a kingdom of their own, history remembers Ferdinand and Isabella as a partnership, co-ruling both realms. This is entirely appropriate; they set the stage for a unified Spain.

ISABELLA SPENT MUCH OF
HER EARLY LIFE AS A VIRTUAL
PRISONER, RECEIVING LITTLE
OF THE FUNDS PROMISED TO
SUPPORT HER.

inherited a weak position that he proved unable
to improve. He sought alliance with Portugal,
marrying Joanna of Portugal after his first
marriage was annulled. This union produced a
daughter who was to be Henry's heir, but the
nobility of Castile favoured his son Alphonso by
his first marriage.

A period of dissent, including a symbolic
deposition of Henry IV and the coronation of his half-brother
Alphonso, resulted in civil war, which was inconclusive. After
Alphonso's death the nobility supported Isabella as their candidate.
The young Isabella had spent her early years as a virtual prisoner
before being summoned to court at the age of 10. Uncertainty had
surrounded her life, but she was not inclined to lead an insurrection.
She declared her support for Henry IV, although she did cast doubt
on the legitimacy of his daughter, Joan. Henry IV named Isabella as
his heir, which was not at all to the liking of his wife.

Throughout Isabella's life she had been used as a pawn
in statecraft, with Henry IV trying to arrange marriages into

Below: The Inquisition
was primarily tasked with
uncovering covert worship
among Jews and Muslims
who had ostensibly
converted to Christianity.
Other forms of heresy
were also to be tackled.

various dynasties.
In 1469, she was
married to Ferdinand
of Aragon without the
agreement of Henry
IV. The ceremony was
held in secret; when
Henry found out, he
reinstated Joan as
his heir. Thus, when
Henry IV died in 1474,
his wife, Joanna of
Portugal, attempted to
put their daughter on
the throne.

This led to a civil
war in which Isabella
was supported by

Aragon as well as most of the Castilian nobility. Her faction was victorious, although she and her husband Ferdinand were required to undertake a lengthy campaign to pacify their realm. Ferdinand was king of Aragon and Isabella of Castile, but they jointly ruled both realms, creating the beginnings of a unified Spain.

In 1480, after peace had been restored, Ferdinand and Isabella implemented the Inquisition. Its role was to root out all forms of heresy, which included variations from the mainstream teachings of the Catholic Church, but also any ostensibly converted Jews or Muslims who continued to practise their old faith. The Inquisition was not universally accepted, with some cities rising in revolt over its imposition.

The year 1492 was important in European – indeed, world – history as the departure date of Christopher Columbus' expedition. Royal patronage had previously been refused, but this time Ferdinand and Isabella agreed. Isabella advocated relatively gentle treatment of the indigenous people discovered by Columbus, and actually rejected the proposal they be enslaved. This attitude was not shared by the Conquistadors who followed Columbus west, however.

Above: Isabella of Castile agreed to fund Christopher Columbus' westward expedition the same year as the reconquest of Iberia was completed. Gold from the New World would bring about a new era of Spanish ascendancy.

This year also saw victory over the last Islamic state in Spain,
completing the Reconquista of the Iberian peninsula, and the
issue of the Edict of Expulsion, which ordered all practising
Jews out of Spain. Those who converted to Catholicism were
permitted to stay, but were always suspected of assisting
converted Jews to secretly practise their faith or even of luring
them back to Judaism.

In 1502, another decree required that all Muslims convert to
Christianity or leave Spain at once. Departure was deliberately
made difficult, however, resulting in a great many Moors
being forced to convert. These former Muslims were known as

Moriscos and were, like former Jews, subject to suspicion and persecution.

Isabella of Castile died in 1504, having created a unified Spain and driven out the enemies of her Church. Her daughter Catherine would marry Henry VIII of England and be mother to Mary I; her grandson Charles was Holy Roman Emperor. In Isabella's lifetime, Castile went from a troubled kingdom to part of a powerful nation that divided the known world with Portugal just as the great age of exploration was beginning. This was the beginning of modern Spain and the creation of a major player in the events of the next centuries.

Left: The siege of Granada brought the reconquest of Iberia to a successful conclusion. Surrender was on relatively generous terms, though failure to observe parts of the agreement led to revolt and necessitated strong military control of the region.

4

PATRONS AND BUILDERS

Many rulers of the medieval period were patrons of art, learning or education – which were often intertwined. Likewise, many of the great buildings of the era were religious in nature. There was a genuine concern among the people of the Middle Ages for the state of their souls; those who could afford it were inclined to fund grand buildings or monasteries where a religious community would pray for their patron's entry to heaven.

GRAND BUILDING projects were also a means of social control. A castle was an obvious sign of a ruler's power, but a cathedral could also exert influence. Not only would it increase the prestige of the ruler's religion, hopefully increasing fervour or gaining new converts, but also it might impress the local population sufficiently so that they were more biddable. To someone living in a rather basic wooden house, a grand stone cathedral might seem quite intimidating; a ruler who could accomplish such a wonder was surely beyond challenge.

Opposite: Grand religious buildings enabled rulers to conduct their ceremonies in appropriate style. Isabella of England was married to Holy Roman Emperor Frederick II at Worms Cathedral.

Some projects appear to have been supported simply out of personal interest, although a wise ruler would be aware of the benefits of a university or similar seat of learning. Not only were such institutions prestigious, but also they would attract the greatest minds of the era, who might then be recruited into the service of the ruler. Students of the institution would also provide an educated class at a time when scholarship was in short supply. The economic and social benefits were considerable, though not always immediately apparent.

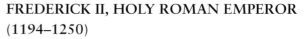

FREDERICK II, HOLY ROMAN EMPEROR (1194–1250)

Patron of learning and trade

Upon the death of Frederick Barbarossa in 1190, his son Henry VI became Holy Roman Emperor and king of Germany. This was not a hereditary position, and although Henry worked to make it so, he was not successful. However, he did manage to defeat a challenge from Henry the Lion, who had been Duke of Bavaria and of Saxony, before being deposed by Frederick Barbarossa.

Above: Henry IV used the ransom he received for Richard I of England's release to fund his campaign against Tancred of Lecce, who attempted to seize the throne of Sicily rather than allowing it to pass to Henry's wife Constance.

Henry VI had a short reign, dying in 1197, but is notable for having gained the crown of Sicily through marriage and being the captor of Richard I of England. The latter was taken prisoner by Duke Leopold V of Austria as he hurried home from crusade to deal with French encroachments on his continental holdings.

Henry VI left behind an infant son, Frederick, who was accepted as king of Germany by its princes. The death of his father endangered the stability of the Holy Roman Empire; despite their recognition of Frederick, the princes of Germany elected two more kings: Otto of Brunswick and Philip of Swabia. Philip came out on top in the resulting power struggle, but was killed in 1208, allowing Otto to become undisputed king of Germany and Holy Roman Emperor.

Frederick was raised by his mother in Sicily, and was crowned king there. Sicily was very troubled at the time, and had not stabilized by the time Frederick married Constance of Aragon in 1209. With her assistance, Frederick was able to pacify Sicily and regain some of the territory that had been lost. He faced a serious threat from Otto, Holy Roman Emperor, who seemed likely to invade Sicily. However, Otto's support among the German princes collapsed and he was deposed in favour of Frederick.

Frederick advanced into Germany, where he fought against Otto's forces from 1212. Otto was on the losing side in the Battle of Bouvines in 1214, which cost him most of his remaining support. By the following year, Frederick had gained control of most of Germany.

Crowned Holy Roman Emperor in 1220, Frederick was finally able to restore the security of Sicily, not least by a programme of fortification building. He also invested in harbours and a merchant fleet, with warships to protect them. Long-term administrative improvements were made with the creation of the University of Naples in 1224 and the development of a civil service making use of its graduates. A few years later, the law regarding the administration of the kingdom was codified and a national constitution created.

Below: At the Battle of Bouvines, Otto IV led an alliance of German, English and Flemish troops against the forces of Philip II Augustus of France. His defeat paved the way for Frederick II to depose him.

Above: Frederick II's court was a seat of learning as well as power. The University of Naples, established under his patronage, attracted great scholars, whilst Frederick took the best graduates into his service.

Frederick was excommunicated in 1227 for failure to keep his earlier promises to go on crusade. He had in fact been making preparations, but delayed his departure due to an outbreak of plague. He departed in 1228, still an excommunicate, and was able to gain control of Jerusalem and other holy cities. His efforts were not appreciated by the Pope, whose forces invaded Sicily. After returning to defeat the papal incursion, Frederick negotiated a reversal of his excommunication.

This was not the end of Frederick's conflict with the papacy. He was again excommunicated in 1239, and ongoing conflict with the Pope and his allies resulted in a need for further administrative reforms to ensure adequate funding. The Pope represented Frederick as a threat to all that was righteous in the world, while Frederick published manifestos in which he presented himself as a new messiah.

FREDERICK II'S SUCCESSFUL LEADERSHIP OF A CRUSADE WHILST STILL EXCOMMUNICATED MUST HAVE POSED A DIFFICULT SPIRITUAL QUANDARY FOR THE POPE.

Upon his death in 1250, legends about Frederick began to circulate. There were claims that he would return some day to counter the corruption of the Church or recreate the Holy Roman Empire. He left behind a legacy of scholarship in Naples, some of which was his own work. Frederick's treatise on falconry was based on his own experience, and the bodies of law and administrative guidelines that he created were derived from his ideas on how a state should be governed.

Below: Edward the Confessor inherited a weak position and was unable to control Godwine, the most powerful of his earls.

EDWARD THE CONFESSOR (1003–1066)

Patron of Westminster Abbey

The Anglo-Saxon kings of England had a long history of patronizing monasteries and religious institutions. Aethelstan, the first to rule over a more or less united England, collected holy relics and gifted them, along with books and money, to monasteries in his realm. The later history of the Anglo-Saxon kings was at times very troubled. Their rule was interrupted by the Danes in 1013–1014 and again in 1016–1042.

Aethelred 'the unready' was driven from his realm in 1016 by Swein Forkbeard of Denmark, but was able to return from exile upon Swein's death. A second Danish invasion, led by Swein's son Cnut, was more successful. Aethelred was in poor health and his realm deeply divided. He died in 1016, his family going into exile in Normandy.

The young Edward (later known as the Confessor) lived in exile until 1042. By that time, Cnut had died and been succeeded by his son, Harald Harefoot. Harald's death in 1040 put his half-brother Harthacnut on the throne. Harthacnut's mother was Emma of Normandy, who had married Cnut after the death of her first husband, Aethelred. Edward the Confessor was thus half-brother to Harthacnut, and his mother was very active in the politics of England. Edward returned from exile to live at the English court, and in 1042 succeeded his half-brother as king of England.

Below: Conflict over the throne of England was resolved at the Battle of Hastings in 1066, depicted here in the Bayeux Tapestry.

Edward's early reign was apparently peaceful, although there were internal troubles. Some of these resulted from favouritism at court and made it difficult for Edward to exert his power as king. Edward's position was threatened by Godwine, Earl of Wessex, who used the king as a figurehead. Edward married Godwine's daughter Edith, but was eventually able to exile the earl in 1051.

However, Godwine was so powerful that he simply returned from exile and demanded to be reinstated. Without the support of a unified kingdom, Edward could do nothing to prevent this.

Godwine's son Harold – later the King Harold who fought at Hastings in 1066 – became an important war leader in Edward's later reign, putting down rebellions and fighting the Welsh. He

WESTMINSTER HALL AND WESTMINSTER ABBEY

WESTMINSTER HALL, now part of the Houses of Parliament in London, was begun by William Rufus, successor to William the Conqueror. It was at the time the largest hall in England, although William Rufus is said to have wanted something even bigger. The hall was used for large occasions; the royal family routinely ate in a smaller room nearby.

By the 1200s, the practice of moving the court around the country had declined, and Westminster Hall became the permanent site of the king's table. This marble edifice was an important symbol of royal power in the next centuries. In 1385, King Richard II commissioned a set of statues representing

Above: Westminster Abbey was conceived by Edward the Confessor, as a rebuilding of the existing St Peter's Abbey in the new Romanesque style.

the monarchs of England, from Edward the Confessor onwards, to be placed in alcoves in the great hall. Richard II was deposed in the hall in 1399, making way for Henry IV to take the throne.

Westminster Abbey was altered by later monarchs. Henry III had the abbey rebuilt in the Gothic style, in part as a burial site for himself and in part to venerate the memory of Edward the Confessor. The present form of the abbey is the result of Henry III's works.

also strongly opposed the growing Norman influence at the Anglo-Saxon court, in opposition to Edward, who had grown up in Normandy.

Edward was undoubtedly a pious man, and his lack of an heir has at times been portrayed as a sign that he was unconcerned with earthly matters. This is unlikely, but for all that Edward and Edith failed to produce an heir. This probably conflicted with the plans laid by Godwine, who must have assumed that he was to be grandfather to the next king of England.

Lack of an heir concerned Edward, who managed to locate the son of his half-brother Edmund Ironside. Edmund's son, Edward the Exile, came to England, but died soon thereafter, leaving the succession still in doubt. There were no absolute rules in place at the time for a disputed succession; blood claims were a factor, but so was the power wielded by the claimant and his level of approval by other lords and the Church. Designation by the monarch was also a valid claim even if no blood relationship existed.

Edward's death in 1066 precipitated a struggle for the throne of England that led to the Norman Conquest. He was immediately succeeded by Harold Godwinson, who first defeated a challenge from Harald Hardrada of Norway in alliance with rebel English nobles, then marched to meet the invasion led by Duke William of Norway. He was killed at the Battle of Hastings, and William was crowned William I of England.

THERE WERE NO CLEAR RULES FOR SUCCESSION IN 1066 — POWER, BLOOD RELATIONS OR DESIGNATION BY THE CURRENT MONARCH WERE ALL FACTORS.

Edward was given the nickname 'the Confessor' to reflect the status he was given as a near-saint. He did not suffer martyrdom as an earlier Edward of England (Edward the Martyr) did, but was canonized in 1161. His greatest contribution to religion in England was the construction of Westminster Abbey, where he was eventually buried.

Westminster Abbey became the traditional place of coronation for English monarchs, much as the cathedral at Reims was in France. It is possible that Harold Godwinson was crowned there; William I (William the Conqueror) was. Other religious events concerning the English royal family, such as weddings and funerals, have also traditionally been conducted at Westminster.

Westminster Abbey was the first great religious building in England built in the Norman style. As the burial place of the last Anglo-Saxon king and the first Norman monarch of England, its construction marked a new era in the history of England.

ROGER II OF SICILY (1095–1154)

Cosmopolitan patron of learning, culture and trade

The fusion of Norse and Frankish culture in Normandy produced some of the finest fighting men Europe had to offer in the early Middle Ages. Norman mercenaries were favoured in many states, and their own expeditions resulted in the creation of Norman kingdoms far from their homeland. The most notable of these was the Norman kingdom of Sicily.

Norman adventurers were highly active in Italy during the mid-eleventh century. Along with other family members, William de Hauteville campaigned against Byzantine rule in Calabria in the south of Italy and became Count of Apulia in 1042. Roger Guiscard, half-brother to William, arrived in 1047, and eventually acquired Apulia. He was joined in 1057 by his brother, the future Robert I of Sicily, and together they succeeded in gaining full control of the region.

THE FIERCE ENERGY OF THE NORMANS LED TO ADVENTURERS CARVING OUT REALMS IN THE MEDITERRANEAN AND MAINLAND ITALY.

The brothers began a conquest of Sicily in 1061, capturing Palermo in 1072. Sicily had been a centre for sea trade around the Mediterranean for centuries, largely due to its strategic location, and Palermo was a rich prize. Roger was given control of Sicily and Calabria as a vassal to Robert Guiscard, and after Robert's death Roger I became independent. He was recognized as head of the Sicilian Church in 1098.

Roger I died in 1101. He had several children by three marriages, but was succeeded by Simon, his eldest child by his third wife. Simon died in 1105, leaving the nine-year-old Roger

II to inherit with his mother as regent. Roger began ruling in his own right in 1112, making Palermo his capital.

Roger II was a very different man from his father, who was thoroughly Norman in all ways. The young Roger II, however, had grown up in multicultural Sicily and southern Italy, with Greek and Muslim influences. Whereas his father had been an adventurer and a warrior, Roger II was a diplomat first and foremost. This approach seems to have served him better than the straightforward methods of the Normans; the descendants of Robert Guiscard ran into a series of troubles on the mainland that Roger II was able to quietly exploit. In return for supporting them and dealing with the occasional crisis on their behalf, Roger gradually acquired land from his relatives. By 1122, he was the ruler of Calabria as well as Sicily.

Above: Roger I of Sicily was a straightforward Norman fighting-man. He laid the groundwork for the Kingdom of Sicily, but it was his son Roger II's diplomacy that ensured it prospered.

In 1127, Roger inherited the Duchy of Apulia, although not without opposition. In particular, the Pope did not want a powerful and united Norman state in southern Italy. Bargaining from a position of great strength, Roger overcame opposition from Pope Honorius II and was recognized as Duke of Apulia, Calabria and Sicily. Upon the death of Honorius II, two candidates were elected, leading to schism within the Church. Roger II sided with Antipope Anacletus II in return for recognition as king of Sicily. He was crowned in 1130.

The schism resulted in war, and even after the death of Anacletus Roger fought against Pope Innocent II, Anacletus' opponent. After capturing the Pope, Roger forced him to confirm his coronation, then set about restoring stability to his mainland Italian possessions.

As king, Roger II made the most of the assets he had to hand. His own characteristically Norman energy was brought to bear on many tasks, including personal oversight of financial matters. He drew on the strengths of multicultural Sicily – the Greek affinity for maritime warfare and trade, Arab learning and financial aptitude, and Norman energy. His kingdom was run by a civil service created for the purpose, using methods chosen for effectiveness rather than traditional ways.

Roger's court attracted scholars from many nations, creating a place where Muslim, Greek and Western European

Below: Pope Innocent II's opposition to Roger II was brought to an end when the Pope tried to play Roger at his own game and was captured northwest of Naples by Roger's troops.

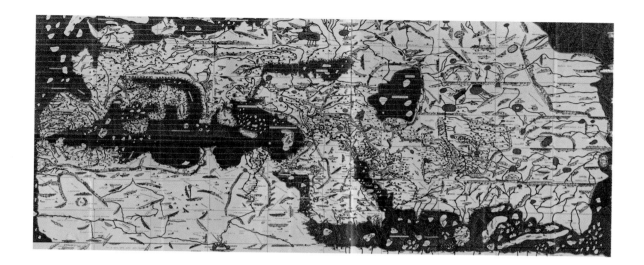

ideas were exchanged to mutual benefit. This was particularly unusual in an era when the crusades were causing hatred and division elsewhere. Notably, the kingdom of Sicily did not take part in the Second Crusade.

King Roger II funded the construction of many great buildings, some of which show very diverse cultural inspiration. He paid particular attention to financial matters, streamlining his currency to facilitate long-distance trade. His powerful navy protected merchant shipping, but also engaged in profitable maritime expeditions – a trait perhaps inherited from Roger's Norse ancestors.

Sicilian vessels landed expeditions in Greece and Tunisia, raiding for profit and occasionally annexing territory. In these endeavours, Roger's mariners were aided by the excellent mapmaking skills of scholars at court and the extensive body of knowledge brought by scholars from all over the Mediterranean.

Roger II died in 1154, having fostered a unique Norman/Arab/Byzantine culture in his realm and created a place of great learning and scholarship. Although aged only 58, he accomplished much due to his personal energy and drive; it was said of him that he could do more in his sleep than others did in a whole day.

Above: Roger II had some of the finest mapmakers in Europe in his realm. He made good use of their skills, complemented by the Greek talent for sailing, to facilitate maritime trade and warfare.

THE KINGDOM OF SICILY WAS A FUSION OF NORMAN AND MEDITERRANEAN CULTURES, REFLECTED BOTH IN LEARNING IN PRACTICAL APPLICATIONS.

POPE HONORIUS II AND PAPAL SCHISM

SCHISM WITHIN THE CHURCH occurred upon the death of Pope Calixtus II in 1124. A controversial election produced two Popes, each backed by a faction in the Church. Honorius II emerged as the legitimate Pope, with his rival Celestine II declared an Antipope. Honorius II led a coalition against Roger II of Sicily in an effort to break up the emerging powerful Norman state in southern Italy. Defeated, he agreed to recognize Roger's status instead, receiving an oath of fealty from the new Duke Roger of Apulia.

Honorius died in 1138, and again schism produced two Popes. Anacletus II was supported by the majority of cardinals and also possessed greater military support. His rival, Innocent II, relocated to France. By a combination of political pressure and military action, Innocent II eventually established himself as the legitimate Pope, making Anacletus II Antipope. This outcome is still debated by some scholars.

HONORIVS · II · PAPA · BONONIÆ·

166

Left: Roger II of Sicily attempted to annex territories promised to the Church by his cousin, William of Apulia, bringing him into conflict with Pope Honorius II.

BELA IV OF HUNGARY (1206–1270)

Creator of a strong and stable Hungary

The balance of power between monarchs and the nobility shifted throughout the Middle Ages. Overall, a general trend existed towards a more even balance of power, making the internal politics of late medieval states more complex. However, this trait was not universal or constant; local and short-term variations occurred throughout the era.

During the reign of Andrew II of Hungary (1177–1235), the position of the king relative to his nobles was weak. Facing plots among the nobility, Andrew's position was not improved by pressure from the Pope to lead a crusade. His father, Bela III, had agreed to do so and the responsibility now fell on Andrew II. Financing the endeavour required selling off royal estates and privileges, and making deals that traded yet more royal property for transportation and support.

Andrew II thus took part in the Fifth Crusade, returning to an impoverished and chaotic Hungary in 1218. In 1222, the nobility forced Andrew to issue the Golden Bull, a declaration that has been compared to England's Magna Carta. The Golden Bull set out the rights and prerogatives of the nobility and the limits on royal power. Among its provisions was the requirement that noblemen be given a fair trial rather than being imprisoned at the king's whim. The nobility could also no longer be required to provide military service without payment. These provisions were backed up by a declaration that the nobility and clergy could not be considered traitors if they rose in resistance to a king who failed to abide by the terms of the Golden Bull.

Below: Andrew II of Hungary issued the Golden Bull, a document similar in magnitude and content to the English Magna Carta.

II. ANDRÁS
1205 – 1235

Opposite: The Hungarian army inflicted a sharp defeat on the Mongol advance guard at the Sajó River but then failed to secure the bridge, allowing them to cross.

Below: Bela IV was fortunate not to lose his realm to the first Mongol invasion, but ensured that future incursions were met with a stubborn defence.

IV. BÉLA
1235 – 127

Pressure from the nobility resulted in Andrew's son Bela being crowned in 1214, against his father's wishes. Bela inherited the kingdom of Hungary as Bela IV in 1235, finding it in a deplorable state. His first task was to restore some of the lands and privileges lost by his father. This was a risky move, as it caused resentment among the nobility at a time when royal power was weak, and was overshadowed by the Mongol invasion of 1241.

After raiding deep into Hungary, the Mongols pulled back, drawing the Hungarian army after them, until they reached the River Sajó. There, the concentrated Mongol force launched an attack that resulted in a disastrous defeat for Bela IV despite initial successes. Hungarian losses were so severe that resistance to the Mongols collapsed. The city of Pest was taken and Bela was forced to flee to Austria. There, he was captured and forced to pay a huge ransom in gold and territory.

Bela IV tried to rally support from the kingdoms of Europe and from the Pope, but little aid was forthcoming. A German army was eventually assembled, but the Mongols began to withdraw eastwards before any real action was taken. The reasons for this remain unclear, and there may have been no single cause. Great Khan Ogodei had recently died and the Mongol leaders needed to be present at the election of his successor, but there is some evidence that word of Ogodei's death had not reached Hungary at the time of the withdrawal.

The Mongol forces were also overstretched and facing rebellions elsewhere. The Mongols were masters of mobility on the strategic as well as the tactical level, and were quite willing to abandon an area and return later when the strategic situation had changed. Refocusing and concentrating forces to deal with problems elsewhere,

il por auoir barbies et la
tris ꝯ aces gadges nin r
orét·ij·latis q̃ orét de la
lumnare q̃ fu de lille de
cyppre ꝯ lautre auoit nõ
boniface de molins qui
fu de la cite deuenise·Q̃nt
le soleac ceturac ot asse
ble son ost de toutes pars
il uint ꝯ se combati auec
les tartres en un leue q̃
est nomes cosadach·Grãt
fu la bataille ꝯ asse; i furet
mors ꝯ dune partie ꝯ eau
tre·Et a la fin les tartres
orét la uictoure ꝯ entre
rent en la tʳe ceturquie
ꝯ la cõquistrét en lan nʳe
seignor·m·CC·xl·iiij·

A pres ce roy ce teṗs octotã
l emperor des tartres mo
rut ꝯ fut fait seignor aṗs
luy un sien fi; qui ot r
guiotã cestui guiotan
uesqui poy ce temps et
aṗres luy fu fait empe
or un sien cosin q̃ auoit
nõ mãgoca qui mlt fu
uaillant ꝯ sage ꝯ asse; a
quist ce tʳes ꝯ ce seigno
ries·A la fin si cõme soup;
ce grãt cuer entra parti
en royaume de cathay·
Et cõme il assegiast une
ille la q̃le il uoloit prendre
par mer la gét de cele tʳe q̃
sont mlt engignors mã
derét homes qui sauoiét
noer ꝯ ceaux entrerent

then launching a new campaign into Europe when the time was right, would have been a logical and sound strategy.

Whatever the reason, the Mongol withdrawal permitted Hungary to re-emerge from the chaos. Uprisings in the provinces taken by Austria allowed Bela IV to reclaim them. The threat of a renewed Mongol incursion now served as a unifying factor. Before the first invasion the danger had been largely discounted and Hungary was caught unprepared. The consequences of that were all too apparent; the previously rebellious nobility were now more inclined to support their king as he worked to strengthen Hungary's defences.

BELA IV OVERSAW A PROGRAMME OF TARGET-HARDENING, ENSURING THAT A REPEATED MONGOL INVASION WOULD FIND NO EASY VICTORIES.

In order to do so, Bela IV decreed that the nobility would henceforth be permitted to construct fortifications; this had previously been a royal prerogative. Similarly, nobles and high-ranking clergymen were permitted to raise and maintain private armed forces. In 1247, the population of Pest was moved to a more defensible site just across the Danube. There, the town of Buda was founded and given defensive works to resist future attacks.

Defence was also secured by alliances and campaigns against neighbouring states. Although not always successful in war, Bela IV led a Hungary that had emerged as a potent force and was confident enough to simply ignore Mongol demands for tribute and forces to assist in a renewed invasion of Europe.

When it came in 1285, the second Mongol invasion of Hungary had a very different outcome to the first. Target hardening in the form of fortifications deprived the Mongols of easy conquest and plunder, while Bela's military reforms had created an army capable of defeating them in battle. Pest was taken and burned, but had already been abandoned, while fortified Buda served as the base for action against nearby Mongol forces.

Bela IV did not live to see these events. He died in 1270 having successfully resisted threats from an increasingly powerful Bohemia. His fortified town at Buda became the capital of Hungary in 1361, eventually uniting with Pest to create the modern city of Budapest.

FEUDALISM

A FEUDAL SOCIETY WAS defined, in general terms, by chains of responsibility and duty running from the highest echelons of society to the lowest. Lands and rights (such as taxation, tolls placed on certain roads or the raising of troops) were granted in return for service and loyalty. In theory, the nobility provided protection, governance and resolution of disputes – i.e. stability – to the common folk, in return for their obedience and payment of taxes. In a feudal society, the amount of time for which a vassal was required to serve was fixed, making it difficult to maintain a long military campaign.

The term 'bastard feudalism' is sometimes used for the situation that occurs when the traditional concept of service is replaced by financial obligations, or more loosely to refer to a society where the nobility have become sufficiently powerful to challenge the authority of the king. Substituting financial obligations for military service grants the ruler greater flexibility, but risks a devolution of power to the point where the monarch must constantly bargain with his subjects rather than issuing orders.

Below: Louis IX reformed the legal system in France, abolishing trial by combat and establishing the presumption of innocence.

CHARLES IV, HOLY ROMAN EMPEROR (1316–1378)

Defined the conditions for succession in the Holy Roman Empire

The Premyslid dynasty of Bohemia dated back to the ninth century, gaining in power despite a variety of setbacks until Duke Vratislaus II was named King of Bohemia in 1085. The throne was not at that time hereditary, but over the ensuing centuries the Premyslid dynasty became well established as rulers of Bohemia.

The discovery of silver ore greatly increased Bohemian wealth from the end of the thirteenth century. King Wenceslaus II was also king of Poland and Hungary, although Bohemian control over these states was lost soon afterwards, and upon the death of Wenceslaus III in 1305 the Premyslid dynasty came to an end. Wenceslaus III was intending to launch a campaign into Poland with the aim of re-establishing control over areas that had been lost when he was murdered by an unknown assailant.

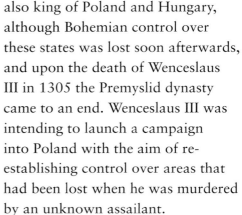

The death of Wenceslaus III led to a period of conflict until Count John of Luxembourg was elected king. John was the son of Henry VII, Holy Roman Emperor. He married Elizabeth of Bohemia, daughter of Wenceslaus II, and in 1316 they had a son. He was named Wenceslaus, but would take the regnal name Charles upon becoming Holy Roman Emperor and king of Hungary.

The young Charles had a difficult upbringing. His father was unpopular in his adopted homeland, and at odds with Elizabeth. In 1323, Charles was sent to the court of King Charles IV of France. Charles died without an heir and was succeeded by Philip IV, although Edward III of England also had a claim to the throne. This was the beginning of a dispute that would grow into the Hundred Years' War.

Below: Wenceslaus III, king of Hungary, Bohemia and Poland, lost large areas of Poland to Wladyslaw the Elbow-High.

KING OF THE ROMANS

THE TITLE 'King of the Romans' was given to the elected king who ruled over the German princes. The use of the word 'Romans' in this context can be confusing, but in that era it had connotations of nobility and worthiness – i.e. the successors of the great Roman Empire rather than citizens of it or of Rome. Traditionally, the coronation of the King of the Romans took place in Aachen Cathedral.

Initially, the title was used by an elected king who had not yet been crowned as Holy Roman Emperor, but later was used to denote the heir apparent to the imperial crown. The Holy Roman Emperor was crowned by the Pope and had to meet additional criteria such as taking oaths to protect the Church. Once the candidate was ready he journeyed to Italy, where he received the Iron Crown of Lombardy before finally being crowned Holy Roman Emperor in Rome. In several cases an emperor had to wait years for his coronation, especially if there were political issues or military matters to attend to first. Thus, some Holy Roman Emperors are noted as being such several years before their coronation date.

In 1329, Charles married Philip's half-sister, Blanche, who would be his consort for the first few years of his reign until her death in 1348. In the meantime, Charles served his father, John of Bohemia, as a diplomat, administrator and occasional war leader. Suspicion was rife in the plot-wracked court of Bohemia, causing John to mistrust his son while coming to depend ever more upon his talents. As his eyesight failed, John of Bohemia had to rely entirely upon Charles.

In his youth, Blind King John had supported the election of Louis of Bavaria as Louis IV, Holy Roman Emperor. However, they found themselves on opposite sides when the Hundred Years' War broke out in 1337. Louis sided with England, while John had strong ties with France. Louis was also at odds with Pope Clement VI, whereas John's son Charles had been taught by him in France before his election to the papacy. John secured the support of the Pope in deposing Louis as Holy Roman Emperor. Charles was elected in his place, becoming King of the Romans in 1346.

Right: Charles IV was a skilled diplomat, who secured stability in his realm and even expanded it by peaceful means.

Soon afterwards, both Charles and his father John took part in the disastrous Battle of Crécy. King John was killed, having joined the fighting despite his blindness, but Charles was able to escape. He then faced opposition from Louis of Bavaria, who did not accept his deposition. Even after Louis' death in 1347, a succession of leaders emerged until Charles finally pacified Germany by diplomacy.

Upon becoming king of Bohemia in 1347, Charles redefined the position as hereditary, with succession through the firstborn male and, if no male heir existed, through the female line. At the time Charles had no male heir, but two daughters by his wife Blanche.

A second marriage to Anne of Bavaria produced a short-lived son, and after Anne's death in 1353 he married a third time. His new wife, Anna von Schweidnitz, bore him two children before dying in childbirth with a third. Their daughter, Elizabeth of Bohemia, married Duke Albert of Austria and his son Wenceslaus succeeded his father as King of the Romans (i.e. king of Germany) until deposed in 1400. Wenceslaus retained the throne of Bavaria until his death in 1419. Charles' fourth wife was Elizabeth of Pomerania, granddaughter of Casimir the Great of Poland. Four of their six children survived. The eldest, Anne of Bohemia, married Richard II of England; the second was Sigismund, later Holy Roman Emperor.

By 1355, Charles had been crowned with the Iron Crown of Lombardy as well as the imperial crown of the Holy Roman Empire. In addition to ensuring the place of Bohemia as a major player in European politics, Charles IV was a patron of

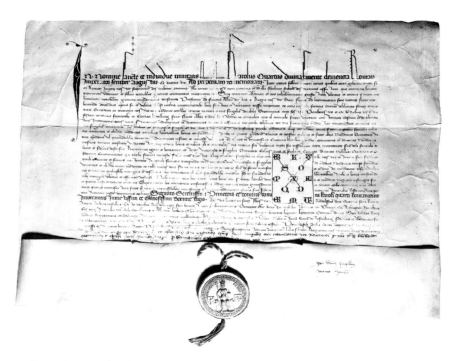

Left: The Golden Bull of Charles IV set out the conditions for succession to the imperial crown. It clearly defined the seven electors' privileges and their status relative to the king of Bohemia.

education and a builder of great works. He founded the first university in central Europe to rival those of France and Italy, and built castles to secure his holdings. However, his most notable lawmaking was the Golden Bull of 1356.

The Golden Bull laid out the conditions for succession to the imperial throne. The emperor would be elected by seven electors. Four were secular princes, three were ecclesiastical princes, and all were subordinate to the king of Bohemia. This paved the way for Charles' son Wenceslaus to be elected as Holy Roman Emperor, although the process was not without difficulties. Charles IV died in 1378, and was succeeded by his son Wenceslaus IV.

PHILIP THE GOOD OF BURGUNDY (1396–1467)

Patron of chivalry, master of the greatest court in Europe

Burgundy was founded as a kingdom by migrating Germanic tribesmen during the Völkerwanderung period. It was subsequently incorporated into the Frankish kingdom as a duchy, but remained influential in French affairs, with the duke of Burgundy often a rival or an opponent of the king of France.

Philip I of Burgundy died in 1361 as a very young man, without heirs. Accounts of his death vary, but the outcome was that Burgundy became a possession of the French crown. It was given to Philip, the youngest son of King John II of France, in 1363. Philip had earned himself the nickname 'the Bold' during the Battle of Poitiers in 1356, where he was captured along with his father. He was a prisoner for a time and upon his release was given the duchy of Touraine, but relinquished it to become Duke of Burgundy.

After the death of King John II, Philip the Bold was one of four great dukes forming a council of regents. Along with the Dukes of Anjou, Berry and Bourbon, he was uncle to the young Charles VI, John's successor. Philip more or less ruled France at this time, and when Charles eventually asserted his own leadership he inherited a difficult situation. The Hundred Years' War, although it was not known by that name at the time, was ongoing and presented a constant drain on the treasury. The council of regents had also used royal funds for their own endeavours, and sometimes to thwart one another. Weariness at high taxation was also causing unrest.

THE RANSOM OF KING JOHN II OF FRANCE WAS A BONE OF CONTENTION BETWEEN ENGLAND AND FRANCE FOR MANY YEARS.

Charles was sufficiently successful and popular that he became known as 'the Beloved', but soon earned himself the nickname of 'the Mad'. After 1392, he was prone to bouts of madness and even when sane he was troubled to the point that he could not govern effectively. Again, Philip the Bold became regent, triggering a power struggle with Louis, Duke of Orleans. He had lost and regained the position of regent by the time of his death in 1404.

Philip the Bold was succeeded by his son, John, who earned himself the nickname 'the Fearless' during the disastrous crusade to Nicopolis in 1396. In addition to the duchy of Burgundy, John inherited his father's position in French politics. He continued to contest control of the insane Charles VI with Louis of Orleans, finally sending assassins to kill Louis. This did not end the power struggle, and in addition to internal troubles France had to deal with an invasion by the English king, Henry V.

Opposite: King John and his son Philip were captured by the English at the Battle of Poitiers; one of the three great clashes of the Hundred Years' War along with Crécy and Agincourt.

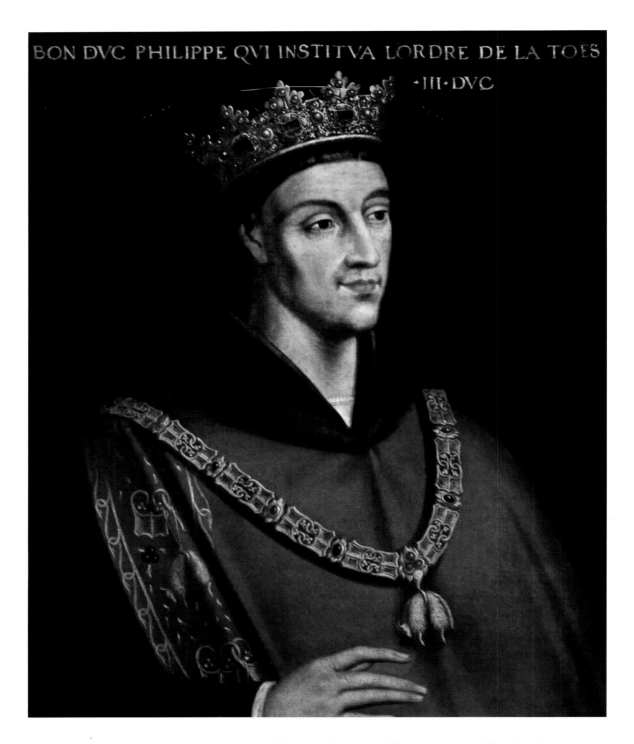

BON DVC PHILIPPE QVI INSTITVA LORDRE DE LA TOES
·III·DVC

Above: Philip the Good declined membership of the English Order of the Garter, instead founding his own Order of the Golden Fleece. Most of its members were not permitted to join other knightly orders.

John the Fearless was one of those who encouraged Henry V to claim the French throne, and although he mustered his army in response to the invasion his forces did not arrive in time to take part in the Battle of Agincourt in 1415. After Agincourt, France was beset by political infighting, with the English in possession of large areas of territory. John seized control of Paris, although he was not able to prevent the escape of the Dauphin, the future Charles VII. In 1419, the two met to agree terms, but at their second meeting John was assassinated.

The duchy of Burgundy then passed to John's son Philip ('the Good'). With the control of Charles VI, Philip was able to agree the Treaty of Troyes with Henry V in 1420. Under its terms, the Dauphin would be disinherited and the throne of France would go to Henry upon the death of Charles. The Dauphin did not find this acceptable and continued to fight for the French crown. In this he was greatly assisted by Joan of Arc, although once he had succeeded in taking the throne he gave her little support. Joan of Arc was captured by Burgundian forces and handed over to the English for trial as a heretic.

Above: John the Fearless met the Dauphin on the bridge of Montereau under what were supposed to be carefully controlled diplomatic conditions. The Dauphin's escort probably intended to attack John's party from the outset.

Philip's alliance with England was always opportunistic. In 1435, he accepted Charles VII as king of France and broke his alliance with England. This lasted until 1439, when Philip changed sides again. Attempting to use a foreign state as a tool in his own schemes was a risky strategy, but Philip was largely successful. He added greatly to his lands, annexing some territory by force and other areas by diplomatic or economic means. Philip purchased Luxembourg in 1443 from Elizabeth of Bohemia; she had received it when Sigismund of Bohemia and Hungary, Holy Roman Emperor, was unable to pay the mortgage he had raised on the territory.

AN OPPORTUNIST, PHILIP THE GOOD PLAYED THE CARDS HE WAS DEALT VERY WELL, GREATLY INCREASING THE WEALTH AND POWER OF BURGUNDY.

Acquisition of territory in the Low Countries made Philip a natural patron for Flemish artists, notably Jan van Eyck, who was sent to Portugal on behalf of Philip. His mission was to paint an accurate portrait of Isabella, daughter of King John of Portugal, to whom Philip was considering marriage. Numerous other artists were employed at Philip's court, which moved around his extensive territory as necessary.

Philip's court was ostentatious in the extreme, living up to or exceeding the popular image of opulence in the Middle Ages. Accounts of the Feast of the Pheasant, held in 1454 to commemorate Philip's decision to go on crusade, speak of musicians playing inside a giant model pie and of extravagant entertainment for the guests. Although the crusade was never launched, the intention was probably sincere. The name of the feast came from the oaths taken on a live pheasant; bird oaths were a feature of French chivalry at the time.

Philip was also a patron of chivalry, holding tournaments for entertainment and also as a tool of statecraft. He founded the knightly order of the Golden Fleece, whose membership was restricted to 24 of the most notable knights in Europe. Philip died in 1467, leaving behind an expanded duchy of Burgundy that was a major player in the politics of Europe and home to industries producing an array of luxury goods.

PATRONS OF KNOWLEDGE IN TROUBLED TIMES

HENRY VI OF ENGLAND (1421–1471) was a good and pious man, which was enough to make him unsuited to ruling England even without his propensity for fits of madness. His weakness as king was one of the factors leading to the dynastic struggle known as the Wars of the Roses. As a patron of education and religion, however, Henry was rather more successful. He founded Eton College and had commissioned its chapel, although the project had to be amended when funding dried up due to Henry's disposition. Similarly, he founded King's College at Cambridge and ordered work to begin on its chapel. All Souls College at Oxford was also founded by Henry VI.

Henry VI's wife, Margaret of Anjou, was made of sterner stuff than her husband and at times led the Lancastrian faction or essentially ruled the country while her husband was incapacitated. The two had little in common except for their patronage of education. Margaret of Anjou founded Queen's College at Cambridge in 1448; after her downfall, Elizabeth Woodville, consort to King Edward IV of England, refounded the college.

Right: Margaret of Anjou was one of the major players in the Wars of the Roses, whereas her husband Henry VI was little more than an observer or even a victim much of the time.

5

LAWMAKERS

The Middle Ages saw the rise of increasingly large kingdoms, the management of which required well-defined sets of laws and customs. For much of the era, the word of the king was law, but even this institution was challenged in some areas.

LAWS SHAPED the society of their nation, often in subtle ways. Rules about succession and the passing of power from one monarch to the next were of great importance – disagreements with the existing practice could lead to revolt or even civil war, but so could blindly following a rule that put a qualified but totally unsuitable candidate on the throne. Likewise, the absence of rules covering an unusual situation, such as where a king outlived all his close relatives, could plunge a previously stable realm into chaos.

Other laws had less immediate but equally important ramifications. In some regions, members of the clergy were protected from even the king's justice, and holy ground was a sanctuary. The violation of this sanctuary to seize a fleeing enemy prompted a change in the laws at the end of the English Wars of the Roses – a loophole was quietly created to the effect

Opposite: The relationship between religion and state was a complex one, and Church officials were in many ways beyond the reach of secular law. A ruler needed the approval of the Church, but could not afford to be subordinate to it.

Above: Like many medieval rulers, Henry II moved around his realm, holding court wherever he went. Access to the royal court was limited, with many petitioners waiting for days, only to be denied an audience.

that a traitor against the crown was not subject to the normal rules of sanctuary. This removed one possible way the Church and monarch might be drawn into a conflict that neither wanted, but had implications for those accused of treason in the future.

Many of the kings of Europe are remembered as lawmakers, or in some cases as the reason why laws were made. A code of laws, once established, was a powerful legacy that might be amended, but was unlikely to be completely discarded. Thus, practices and laws codified in the Middle Ages are in some cases still in force today.

KING JOHN OF ENGLAND (1166–1216)
Signed the Magna Carta at the insistence of his barons
John was the youngest son of Henry II of England, and was born at a time when English power on the continent was at its greatest. Reportedly, John was his father's favourite; his older brother, Richard, was favoured by their mother, Eleanor of Aquitaine. As a boy, John could have had little expectation of becoming king. He was the youngest of five sons born to Eleanor and Henry, and although the eldest, William, died at the age of three, the others survived their childhood.

Their next child, known as Henry the Young King, was crowned during his father's lifetime, a custom dating back to the Frankish kings of the Merovingian dynasty. He was a popular figure on the tournament circuit, although apparently unsuited to wielding power. In 1173, he led a revolt against his father, in which his mother was also implicated. Eleanor of Aquitaine was imprisoned, but Henry returned to his father's service. This did not last; in 1183, Henry the Young King died of dysentery while fighting against his father's forces in France.

Henry II's fourth son, Geoffrey, was also involved in the revolts of 1173–74 and 1183. Like his brother he was reconciled with his father after the first, but remained discontent. He earned the enmity of the Church by raiding holy buildings for funds to support his wars, and there are versions of the circumstances surrounding his death that suggest divine retribution. Other tales say he was killed in a tournament accident; either way, he died in 1186.

This left Henry II with two sons, John and Richard, when he died in 1189. Richard released his mother from imprisonment and made her his regent when he departed on crusade. The tale

Below: Richard I of England was more concerned with crusading than ruling his kingdom. Whilst popularly portrayed as a beloved king, in counterpoint to his brother John, he was responsible for heavy taxes to pay for his wars and even his ransom.

of Robin Hood has John oppressing the people of England and Richard as the popular king whose return is eagerly anticipated, but in truth John was not regent at this time. For his part, Richard I spent perhaps six months of his reign in England. For the remainder he was on campaign, crusading or imprisoned by the Holy Roman Emperor.

John did attempt a coup while Richard I was imprisoned in Germany, and was exiled for a time when the king was finally ransomed in 1194. Richard had named his nephew Arthur as heir, but in 1196 – with Arthur a captive of the king of France – John was designated instead.

Below: King John made himself highly unpopular at home, a situation exacerbated by defeats on the continent, but at least he was actually present to govern his realm – however poorly.

Richard I died in 1199, and war with France broke out almost immediately. This was largely as a result of John interfering in French politics and taking Isabella of Angoulême as his second wife despite her betrothal to Hugh de Lusignan. Ultimately, John was summoned to pay homage to Philip II of France, which as a noble with holdings in France he was required to do regardless of his status as king of England. He refused, giving Philip II a pretext to renew his attempts to drive the English out of France. In this, Philip was highly successful.

JOHN'S REIGN WAS A DOWNWARD SPIRAL, RESULTING FROM POOR FOREIGN POLICY. WARS REQUIRED HIGHER TAXATION, BUT DEFEAT DID NOT INSPIRE LOYALTY.

Continued wars with France required John to raise additional funds through harsh taxation, which made him increasingly unpopular. A dispute with the Pope over the election of a new Archbishop of Canterbury resulted in excommunication. Although this did permit John to squeeze money out of Church properties for a time, ultimately he was forced into a reconciliation with the Pope. Excommunication was lifted in 1213 by the archbishop whose candidacy John had tried to veto.

Having made peace with the Pope, John was able to concentrate on his conflict with Philip II of France. However, the religious men who wrote the histories were less forgiving, and ensured that John's already suspect reputation would be further tarnished by unsympathetic chroniclers.

John's barons, too, were increasingly weary of his use of royal prerogatives to raise funds for his fruitless French wars. The defeat of John's continental allies at the Battle of Bouvines in 1214 further dented his prestige, and in 1215 the barons rose in rebellion against him. With his enemies in possession of London, John agreed to negotiate, leading to the signing of the Magna Carta.

Among the provisions of the Magna Carta was the extremely important principle that the king was no longer above the law. There were also limitations on taxation and protection against imprisonment or other punishments except in accordance with the law. John soon tried to go back on his word, however, claiming that the Magna Carta was invalid as it had been signed under duress.

The Pope declared the Magna Carta illegal and unjust, and excommunicated the barons who had forced its signing. Open conflict resulted, during which the barons invited Louis, son of Philip II of France, to come to England and assume the throne. John died in 1216 and was succeeded by his nine-year-old son, who became Henry III. The Barons' War came to an end the following year, partly due to loss of support for Louis VIII and partly due to English command of the Channel making it difficult to bring reinforcements across from France. A modified form of the Magna Carta was incorporated into the treaty that ended this conflict.

Below: Henry III, son and successor of King John, did not progress around the kingdom as much as previous monarchs, preferring to move between a small number of royal residences.

pres Jon regna Henry le terz sun fiz. lvi. aunz. si fust de. rx. aunz de age quant fust coione. @ eueu

EDWARD I OF ENGLAND (1239–1307)
Legal and Parliamentary reformer
King John of England died in 1216, to be succeeded by his young son as Henry III. Although the Barons' War between John and the nobility of England was brought to a successful conclusion, Henry III was left to deal with the aftermath. This included the original Magna Carta and its modified form, which was incorporated in the peace settlement. Support for the Magna Carta was a useful bargaining point in gaining concessions from the barons, including the right to raise the additional taxes that Henry needed.

Henry was an unpopular king, a situation made worse by his failures to reconquer lands lost to France. After an unsuccessful campaign to France, he faced a revolt in 1232. Another attempt to invade France a decade later resulted in failure once again, and in 1258 the barons revolted a second time. They were successful in forcing upon Henry reforms known as the Provisions of Oxford.

Despite a peace agreement with France, in which Henry gave up all other claims in return for guarantees of the security of

MAGNA CARTA

Left: The Magna Carta imposed legal restrictions on royal power. Previously, the only real limit was what the nobility was prepared to tolerate before resorting to armed rebellion.

THE MAGNA CARTA LIBERATUM, generally referred to as the Magna Carta, imposed limits on the power of the English king, who had previously been free to imprison anyone he pleased and to raise whatever taxes seemed desirable. It had its origins in the Charter of Liberties proclaimed by Henry I upon his coronation in 1100.

After the disastrous loss of territories in France, King John was at odds with his barons and had little support. He attempted to obtain the assistance of the Pope, not least by vowing to go on crusade, but, with the barons in open rebellion, John was forced to negotiate. The result was the signing of the first Magna Carta at Runnymede in 1215.

Later versions of the Magna Carta were confirmed by other monarchs, beginning with Henry III in 1217 at the end of the First Barons' War. Henry repeated the charter in 1225 in return for the barons' agreement to new taxes; this is the definitive version used in English law. In 1297, Edward I confirmed the Magna Carta as statute law.

The Magna Carta was largely concerned with the rights and protections of the barons themselves, but contained provisions that protected commoners from injustice. It became enshrined in English law, although it was gradually superseded by later laws, and inspired bodies of law in other nations concerned with the protection of individuals from the power of tyrants.

Gascony, Henry's reign in England remained unstable. In 1263, the Second Barons' War broke out, with the opposition to Henry led by Simon de Montfort. Henry was captured, but his son, the future Edward I, escaped from captivity at the hands of the barons and ultimately defeated Simon de Montfort.

Edward participated in the Eighth Crusade, but returned home upon the death of his father to assume the throne. His reign was characterized by wars against the Scots, but his first opponents were the Welsh. In 1277, Edward I launched a successful campaign into Wales, instigating a programme of castle-building to secure the territory. A second campaign in 1282 proved necessary before Wales was pacified. Edward set up an administrative and legal apparatus to govern the region and began moving English settlers into new towns. His son, the future Edward II, was born in Wales and given an appropriate title; since that time, the crown prince of England has always been given the title Prince of Wales.

Disputes over succession to the Scottish throne led to the installation of John Balliol in 1292. Balliol was Edward's favoured candidate, but he could not resist interfering in the affairs of Scotland. Demands that Scottish knights serve in Edward's campaigns against France, along with other unacceptable requirements, resulted in war between England and Scotland. Edward was particularly savage in his campaign, even by the standards of an era when ravaging the land was an accepted part of warfare, and inflicted a serious defeat on the Scots at Dunbar in 1296.

Edward believed the Scots to be crushed, but within a year conflict had broken out, with the Scots now led by William Wallace. An English defeat at Stirling Bridge in 1297 was avenged at Falkirk the following year, but the Scots remained defiant even after the capture and execution of Wallace. The war went on under Robert the Bruce, with conflict continuing after the death of Edward I.

Edward I was harsh in his treatment of England's Jews, taxing them mercilessly

EDWARD I IMPOSED A NEW LEGAL SYSTEM ON HIS TERRITORY IN WALES IN AN EFFORT TO CREATE LASTING STABILITY.

EDWARD I IS REMEMBERED AS A
WARRIOR KING, BUT HIS WARS
REQUIRED ADMINISTRATIVE
CHANGES TO ASSURE SUFFICIENT
FUNDS WERE AVAILABLE.

and attempting to force them to convert to Christianity. In 1290, he issued his Edict of Expulsion, requiring all Jews to leave England. Naturally, this permitted the crown to benefit from the acquisition of their property and outstanding loans. He also imposed heavy taxation upon Church property, prompting a papal bull that forbade the payment of secular taxes by the clergy and another a little later that permitted taxation in some exceptional circumstances.

In addition to imposing a new administrative system on Wales, Edward I reformed English law and reissued the Magna Carta in 1297. Like his predecessor Henry III, Edward did so in return for an agreement that allowed him to raise additional taxation. His reign was characterized by a voracious need for money to fund his wars, which meant that he had to summon Parliament more often than his predecessors.

Edward I made an important change to the way Parliament worked, in that a contingent of commoners was included and, more significantly, were empowered to take part in decision-making. Rather than simply being present to learn what Parliament had decided, commoners now had a share in government.

Edward died in 1307, leaving his son to take the throne as Edward II. Where Edward I had been a strong-willed and temperamental ruler, capable of clinical brutality when necessary, Edward II was more easily led by his favourites. He inherited conflict with Scotland, leading to disastrous defeat at Bannockburn in 1314.

Below: Edward I introduced new coinage, of higher quality than previously, in an effort to combat coin-clipping and to improve confidence in the English currency.

CASIMIR III (THE GREAT) (1310–1370)
Diplomat, negotiator and legal reformer

The Hunnish invasion of Europe left some regions sparsely populated, notably what is today Poland, and from the fifth century onwards Slavic people began to migrate into these areas. Despite incursions by Huns, Avars and other nomadic people, they prospered and built towns that gradually became centres of power. By the late tenth century, a unified state had come to exist, but it fragmented soon afterwards.

By the time of Wladyslaw I (1260–1333), Poland was divided into many small states. Wladyslaw I was elected Prince of Great Poland in 1296, but was later deposed in favour of Wenceslaus II of Bavaria. With the approval of the Pope and assistance from Hungary, Wladyslaw I was able to conquer Little Poland and later Great Poland. He extended his holdings into Pomerania, but lost it in 1308 to the Teutonic Knights. Despite this, Wladyslaw I was crowned king of a reunified Poland in 1320.

Wladyslaw I died in 1333, and was succeeded by his son as Casimir III. Casimir's reign was immediately threatened by

Left: Casimir III was a realist who was willing to renounce his claims to territories that he would not be able to gain control over in return for the security of his existing realm.

neighbouring states that did not recognize him as king of Poland. The nation was also politically isolated, although Casimir's sister Elizabeth was married to the king of Hungary and the king himself was married to the daughter of the duke of Lithuania.

Treading carefully, but with determination, Casimir III negotiated agreements that ensured the stability and security of his kingdom, and conducted military campaigns when the time was right. He was able to add considerable territory to his realm and wisely traded his claims to territory he had no realistic chance of gaining for an agreement with the king of Bohemia that he would, in return, give up his claim on Poland. Success bred success, with some small states agreeing to become vassals of Poland rather than risk forcible annexation.

Although he was a successful warrior, Casimir was first and foremost an organizer. His reform of Poland's military was a factor in some of his victories, and his creation of an improved administrative system contributed to stability and prosperity.

Below: Unusually for the time, Casimir III's laws extended protection to the poor and to Jews. Persecuted elsewhere, a great many Jews came to Poland, with lasting benefits to the economy and educational standards.

Using a system known as Magdeburg Law after the city that pioneered it, Casimir entrusted his cities with self-government, and founded new towns where there would be economic benefits.

A unified body of law was created for Great Poland and Little Poland, although other territories such as Masovia retained their older system. Casimir's body of law was not – as some in the Middle Ages were prone to be – merely about protecting the privileges of the upper classes. He was determined that his laws would protect everyone, including the very poor and Jews. Indeed, Casimir was notable in his positive treatment of Jews at a time when persecution was the norm. Large numbers of Jews came to settle in Poland as a result.

CASIMIR THE GREAT TRANSFORMED POLAND INTO A POWERFUL AND STABLE STATE CAPABLE OF PLAYING A LEADING ROLE IN EUROPEAN POLITICS.

In addition to creating a central court at Krakow, Casimir III encouraged the rule of law by promoting the education of lawyers. The Academy of Krakow was set up for this purpose, also training functionaries and administrators. Casimir's efforts to curb the power of the nobility and to protect the poorest segments of society earned him the nickname 'the peasant king', but he has also been more charitably referred to as the Polish Justinian, after the great Byzantine lawmaker Justinian I.

Casimir III married several times. His first wife, Aldona-Ona, was the daughter of the Grand Duke of Lithuania. The marriage symbolized greatly improved relations between Poland and Lithuania and produced two daughters. Aldona-Ona died in 1339, and in 1341 Casimir entered into a childless marriage with Adelhaid of Hesse. This relationship ended controversially, with Casimir marrying again after a long period of living apart, but without a clear annulment. Casimir's new wife was Christina Rokiczana, a wealthy widow, who also did not provide him with an heir.

At the time of Casimir's marriage to Christina, Adelhaid was still dwelling in Poland and apparently considered she was still married to the king. She protested the situation, with support from the Pope, but Casimir and Christina remained together until

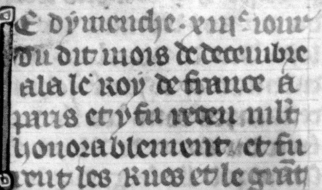

E dymenche .xiii.e iour
du dit mois de decembre
ala le roy de france a
paris et y fu receu mlt
honorablement. et fu
rent les rues et le grãt

around 1264. The following year, Casimir III married Hedwig of Zagan who gave him three children, although only Anne of Poland survived to adulthood.

Casimir III allegedly also had two sons by his Jewish mistress Ezerka, who may be an invention of later historians to explain this attitude towards the Jewish people. The legitimacy of Casimir's children after his first marriage was called into question by Adelhaid, who asserted that his later marriages were bigamous. This problem was solved by persuading the Pope to legitimize the children of Casimir and Christina.

Casimir the Great died in 1370, leaving behind a legacy of castle-building, new towns, religious buildings and children married into the great dynasties of Europe. Although some of his territorial gains were lost after his death he still increased the power and prestige of Poland to an enormous degree. Indeed, in the last years of his life he was asked to arbitrate the disputes of kings – something that would have seemed unlikely three decades earlier.

JOHN II OF FRANCE (1319–1364)

Creator of the French franc

John II, known as John the Good, was the son of Philip VI of France. Philip's succession to the French throne was disputed by Edward III of England, who also had a claim. This led to the conflict known as the Hundred Years' War. In 1346, Philip was defeated at the Battle of Crécy, with heavy casualties among the French nobility, and the Black Death reached France soon afterwards.

John the Good succeeded to the throne upon the death of his father in 1350, inheriting a country that was descending into chaos. Banditry was common, and the Black Death threatened to wipe out whole communities. Meanwhile, war with England continued. Edward, the Black Prince, led a campaign into France in 1355. This was a 'chevauchée', a raid in force to ravage the countryside and cause economic damage, rather than an attempt to capture and hold territory.

JOHN THE GOOD INHERITED A BAD SITUATION, WITH HIS KINGDOM UNDER ATTACK FROM ENGLAND AND SUFFERING INTERNAL DISORDER.

Opposite: John II of France had little chance to make his mark on history. As a result of defeat at Poitiers, much of his reign was spent in captivity in England or trying to raise money to pay his own ransom.

Above: Despite
outnumbering the English
army by a clear margin,
John the Good was
outfought and forced to
surrender along with his
son Philip at Poitiers in
1356. He was treated
with all due respect and
courtesy whilst a captive,
but France suffered for
lack of leadership.

John's army intercepted the English force near Poitiers,
leading to a battle in which John and his son Philip the Bold
were captured. In the hope of avoiding such an occurrence,
the French king surrounded himself with a bodyguard of
knights wearing equipment identical to his own. This ploy
was unsuccessful, although he was able to ensure that his son
Charles escaped captivity.

By all accounts, John fought bravely and well, but was
surrounded and forced to surrender, after which he was treated
with great courtesy. While in captivity in England, John
lived like a king and held his own court. After his capture,
negotiations were conducted between England and Crown
Prince Charles of France, who acted as regent. This was a
complex business, as King John also had to agree any treaty, and
various proposals were rejected by either John or Charles after
the other had agreed them.

King John agreed a treaty with England that ceded vast
territories in addition to an enormous ransom. When this was
rejected by Prince Charles, the English tried to enforce it with

military measures. This failed, and a lesser sum was eventually agreed along with a reduced territorial concession.

Raising the ransom to free John II was a problem for a very troubled France. An attempt to devalue the currency in order to increase the money supply led to unrest in Paris that forced the regent, Prince Charles, out of the capital for a time. This was part of a popular uprising that became known as the Jacquerie after the padded 'jacque' used as armour by the commoners involved in the fighting. The term 'jacquerie' became associated with similar revolts both in England and on the continent.

With France in disarray, John was released in return for other hostages, vowing to raise his own ransom. However, the escape of one of the hostages – John's son Prince Louis – made John feel he was honour-bound to return to England. It has been suggested that he may have preferred the comfortable life of a respected royal guest-in-captivity to struggling with the governance of France. He died in England in 1364. His ransom continued to be paid in instalments, although claims of non-payment remained a bone of contention between England and France for many years to come.

One of the measures implemented to pay the ransom of King John was the creation of the gold franc. It was not possible to mint enough to pay the ransom, but the term 'franc' became associated with money in general. Although France went over to the euro at the beginning of the twenty-first century, some other nations still name their currency francs.

Below: Edward the Black Prince earned glory at the Battle of Crécy in 1346, but his crowning moment was the capture of the French king ten years later at Poitiers. He never ascended to the throne of England.

CHEVAUCHÉE

THE WARFARE OF THE Middle Ages was characterized by sieges of fortified places or large-scale raids intended to cause economic damage and demonstrate a ruler's inability to protect his territory. Known as a chevauchée, a word implying the use of mounted mobility, this mode of warfare was extremely destructive and could force the collapse of a state.

Many of the battles of the Middle Ages occurred as a result of chevauchées. One might be conducted to draw out an enemy and force him to fight, or raiding forces might be intercepted or cut off from their home territory. To the modern eye, such a venture might seem aimless or even pointlessly destructive, but this was an effective tool of warfare used by many rulers to achieve long-term strategic effects. Indeed, the damage caused by a raid might weaken a state or force negotiations in the way that a pitched battle – although resulting in an apparently clear victory – might not. Raids could also be used to damage the enemy without taking the level of casualties resulting from a major battle, and without the risk of disease inherent in siege warfare.

CHARLES V OF FRANCE (1338–1380)
Economic and military reformer

The son and heir of John II, Charles V was left with the unenviable task of governing France while his father was a prisoner in England. He also had to raise an enormous ransom for the king's release at a time when the country was ravaged by both the Hundred Years' War and the Black Death.

At war with both England and Navarre, France was also troubled by popular uprisings and the depredations of out-of-work mercenaries hired by the English for their campaigns in France and then paid off in hostile territory. Defeat at the Battle of Poitiers had further diminished the prestige of the French monarchy, already badly damaged by the Battle of Crécy in 1346.

It was as a supplicant that Charles had to convene the Estates General. This was an assembly composed of representatives of the three 'estates' – the nobility, the clergy and the townsfolk of France. Charles was forced to bargain with the Estates General and grant concessions, promising reforms demanded by the people. There was

Opposite: Charles V ruled France as regent whilst his father was in captivity in England. He faced severe unrest and disaffection in addition to the ravages of the Black Death.

AFTER THE REJECTION OF THE
TREATY OF LONDON BY THE
ESTATES GENERAL, CHARLES
HAD TO RENEGOTIATE WITH THE
UNRECEPTIVE ENGLISH.

Below: The 1360 Treaty
of Bretigny (ratified as
the Treaty of Calais)
rationalized the territorial
holdings of England and
France with the goal of
reducing the chance of
future conflict. The map
shows France in green and
English holdings in red.

sufficient unrest in Paris and the surrounding countryside that Charles had to leave the city in order to raise an army.

In 1359, an attempt was made to settle the dispute with what would be named the Treaty of London. Although initially agreed, the treaty was later rejected by the French Estates General. This was largely because the treaty ceded vast areas of land to England, and also set the ransom of King John at four million gold crowns, which was considered too much.

In 1360, Charles agreed a new settlement with England that ceded large swathes of territory – although less than had originally been demanded – and set the king's ransom at three million gold crowns. The treaty also made provision for territorial exchanges between England and France, with the intention of making the web of feudal responsibilities a little less complex. The process of writing a treaty setting out the exchanges proved long and complex; a process made no easier by English negotiators who preferred the simpler and more profitable 1359 treaty.

The 1360 treaty included an agreement that Edward III of England would renounce his claim to the throne of France. Once it was concluded, a period of peace began, but the ransom was unpaid when John died and Charles ascended the throne of France in 1364. In 1369, war with England broke out again, with the ransom and other treaty obligations arising from the capture of King John among the causes.

Charles' success in the war against England stemmed partly from good strategy and partly from reorganization of his forces. Changes to the way

taxes were raised also improved the ability of France to make war. With the assistance of his Constable, Bertrand du Guesclin, Charles V won a series of victories over his enemies and managed to recover lands lost to both England and Navarre, leading to a new period of stability. Conflict still occurred, but tended to be the result of England and France backing different candidates in succession disputes rather than direct warfare between the two states.

In 1376, the Avignon Papacy came to an end, with Pope Gregory XI returning his seat to Rome after decades in Avignon. Gregory XI died two years later and was replaced by Urban VI, who rapidly offended his cardinals so badly that they decided to replace him. Charles V was a strong supporter of Pope Clement VII, who was elected by the cardinals while Urban VI was still in office.

Clement VII made his seat at Avignon, and had the support of several major states including Castile, Aragon and Scotland. Clement VII and his successors were later declared not to be legitimate and are typically known as Antipopes, but during the Western Schism – as this period was called – Charles' political standing was increased by having the Avignon Pope under his control.

Above: Pope Clement VII brought the papacy back to Avignon. Although later declared an Antipope, at the time he had considerable support among the monarchs of Europe and was widely recognized as legitimate.

ROUTIERS

ROUTIERS WERE BANDS OF mercenary soldiers who were hired out as a unit, or route. At times they gave good service, especially when reliably paid and well led, but they gained a bad reputation for plundering even when in service. When between employers they often engaged in freelance pillaging and banditry. The end of a conflict left large numbers of armed men loose in the countryside, which might be used as a means of causing additional damage to the enemy after the war was concluded.

Large numbers of routiers were employed in the wars between England and France, and by the Holy Roman Emperor. As mercenaries, they had no feudal or state loyalties, and were often willing to chance sides if the price was right. This is one reason why the term 'mercenary' had negative connotations. The lack of loyalties cut both ways – routiers might well be used as fodder by their employers and certainly could not expect them to go to much trouble to ensure the mercenaries' welfare.

Charles V died in 1380, having restored confidence in the currency of France, recovered territories lost as a result of King John's capture, and pacified the country. For his leadership and his patronage of education and learning, Charles gained the byname 'the Wise'. Among his achievements was a refurbishment of the Louvre and the installation of a great library there.

LOUIS XI OF FRANCE (1423–1483)
Well-informed diplomat; harbinger of the French Renaissance
The Middle Ages did not end everywhere all at once. The Renaissance is generally considered to have begun in Italy in the 1450s, gradually spreading across Europe in an uneven manner. Although the Renaissance was a cultural movement first and foremost, it marked a change in the manner of thinking prevalent at the time, with profound social changes. These were made possible by, among other factors, the ravages of the Black Death, which killed so many people that a day's labour became a valuable commodity. As a result, society adapted and the feudal systems of the medieval era gradually morphed into a more modern style of governance.

Opposite: Louis XI ruled France at a time of great change, as the Renaissance spread across Europe. As the old order passed away, those who were well-informed and trod carefully benefited from new opportunities.

Louis XI of France was born just as this process was beginning, at a time when the rule of his father, Charles VII, was weak and facing serious challenges. Louis was thus brought up away from court, in the security of Loches Castle. He was highly educated and trained in the arts of war, but did not have the typical courtly upbringing of a high nobleman of his time. Indeed, his father did not treat him well and his disaffection was completed when Charles VII attended his son's wedding in riding clothes.

LOUIS WAS FREQUENTLY AT ODDS WITH HIS FATHER, CHARLES VII. NEITHER SEEMED PARTICULARLY CONCERNED WITH MAINTAINING GOOD RELATIONS.

A failed attempt to depose his father led to a reconciliation of sorts, and Louis became a war leader for the king. In this he was successful, although he was aware that the end of any conflict freed large numbers of mercenaries to wander around France pillaging wherever they went. For reasons that remain unclear, Louis was recalled to court for a time, before obtaining permission to take over governance of the Dauphiné, a province in southeast France traditionally associated with the crown prince.

Louis made his province something of a personal project, greatly increasing its wealth and reforming its administration, and in 1441 he married the daughter of the Duke of Savoy without permission from his father. This resulted in conflict that almost became open warfare, but Louis was able to obtain sanctuary in Burgundy.

Opposite: A 15th century manuscript depicting Louis XI's arrival in Paris. For his fiscal caution, Louis earned himself the nickname 'the Prudent'; for his diplomacy he became known as 'the Cunning'; and for his scheming he was called 'the Universal Spider'.

Upon the death of his father in 1461, Louis succeeded to the throne. Perhaps due to his unusual upbringing he did not remain at court if he could avoid it; he preferred to travel around the country and seemed to prefer the hospitality of a friendly peasant house to a state occasion. For all of this, he plotted constantly and was well informed about events within and beyond France. Louis defeated an attempt to overthrow him led by his brother the Duke of Berry in 1465, and engaged in adept diplomacy to resolve conflict with Burgundy.

In 1470, Louis entered into an agreement with Richard Neville, Earl of Warwick, to depose Edward IV from the throne

Uant toute ceste
compaignie fut
passee que l'on
estimoit a Cent
ul cheuaulx que bons que
rauuais Ce que se croy
delibererent lesd seigneurs
e partir pour tirer deuant
aris et misdrent toutes le͏s
uantgardes ensemble. pour
es bourguygnons les coduisoit

les ducz de Berry et de Bretai
gne Oudet desser depuis
Conte de Comminges et le
mareschal de Loheac comm
al me semble: Et ainsi s͏e
acheminerent. Tous les p
ces demourerent a la batail
Led conte de Charrolops e
le duc de Calabre prenoient
grand peine de commander
de faire tenir ordre a leurs

of England. The plot succeeded, but led to war with Bur
Louis adopted a strategy of stalling rather than engagin;
decisive battle, and was able to negotiate a new truce. F
the same approach when Edward IV, restored to the thr
of England, invaded France in 1475. Louis' army was r
to fight, but he used it as a bargaining counter rather th
committing it to action.

Victory over Burgundy was won by diplomacy rather
force of arms. Louis negotiated agreements that undermi
Burgundian power and cut off trade revenue, sweeping u
Burgundy and reuniting it with France
the death of its duke, Charles the Bold
the time of his death in 1483, Louis X
reformed the system of government in
paving the way for it to become a Ren
state rather than a feudal monarchy. F
always careful, cunning and diplomati
earning him the byname 'the Prudent'.

JIS' PREFERRED STRATEGY
TO USE HIS MILITARY
ABILITY AS A THREAT WHILST
TRALISING HIS ENEMIES BY
OMACY OR ECONOMIC MEANS.

GEORGE OF PODĚBRADY (1420–1471)
Proponent of European Unity

The execution as a heretic of Jan Hus in 1415 sparked th
conflict known as the Hussite Wars. The Hussites were
subdivided into factions, of whom the Taborites were the
radical and the Utraquists far more moderate. Factionaliz
made a peace settlement particularly difficult, as an agree
acceptable to one group might then be rejected or simply
by another. Eventually this led to inter-faction conflict.

One of the primary opponents of the Hussites was the
Holy Roman Emperor Sigismund, king of Bohemia as we
Germany, Hungary and Croatia. Sigismund died in 1437
succeeded by his daughter Elizabeth. However, she was r
to the role of consort and her husband Albert of Austria
recognized as king.

George of Poděbrady was the son of a Bohemian nobl
affiliated to the Utraquist faction of the Hussites. The you
George fought in the Hussite Wars, notably at the Battle

JOAN OF ARC

JOAN OF ARC WAS a commoner, born in 1412 at a time when the fortunes of France were at a low ebb. The reign of Charles VI began well; he ended the power struggles that had raged between his uncles before he came of age and reformed the economy sufficiently that he was known for a time as Charles the Beloved. Unfortunately, hereditary insanity reversed his good works and he became known as Charles the Mad. The invasion of France by England's Henry V resulted in the Treaty of Troyes in 1420, whereby Henry V and his heirs would rule France after the death of Charles.

This meant that the crown prince, the future Charles VII, was dispossessed and found it difficult to rally sufficient support for a bid to retake his throne. Joan of Arc, claiming divine instructions, went to his court and sufficiently impressed both Charles and the clergy that she was given command of the French forces. Joan retook Reims from the English, enabling Charles VII to be crowned as king of France, but was eventually captured and handed over to the English, who burned her as a heretic and witch. She was subsequently absolved of the charges by the Pope and canonized as a saint.

Left: After regaining his throne, Charles VII seems to have lost interest in supporting Joan of Arc, who was subsequently captured and burned as a heretic by the English.

Lipany, where the radical Taborites and their allies were defeated by the Utraquists and their power broken. Lipany was notable as a clash between two groups making use of the unusual Hussite 'wagenburg' tactic of making forts out of wagons, although in the event the Taborites came out of their mobile fortress to attack their enemies and were defeated by a vigorous counterattack.

George of Poděbrady rose to be a leader among the Hussites, and after the death of Albert of Austria he led the Hussite faction in a struggle for control of Bohemia. He was able to gain control of Prague in 1448, but faced opposition from the traditionally fractious nobility of Bohemia. However, in 1451 Holy Roman Emperor Frederick III conferred governance of the country on George, who was to act as regent for Albert's young son Ladislaus.

Above: George of Poděbrady was named Regent of Bohemia in 1451, and became king six years later. His association with the Hussites brought him into conflict with the Pope, resulting in an invasion by Hungary.

Ladislaus favoured the mainstream Catholic Church rather than the Hussite beliefs of George, which made his sudden death in 1457 seem highly suspicious. However, George of Poděbrady is unlikely to have done him harm and was named king of Bohemia in 1458. Perhaps as a result of growing up in an era of religious civil war, George of Poděbrady hoped to bring peace not just to Bohemia but all across Europe.

The proposal put forward by George of Poděbrady was extremely forward-thinking. He wanted to create a European parliament in which decisions affecting the whole continent could be debated and where differences between member states could be peaceably resolved.

George of Poděbrady's motives were not entirely peaceful, nor were they secular in nature. The Ottoman Empire was at the time encroaching upon his home region; George hoped to create an invincible alliance of Christian states that would not be weakened by internal divisions and conflicts to oppose the Ottoman threat. Thus, although he was proposing a sort of 'European Union', it was a religious rather than secular organization.

George of Poděbrady respected and observed the Compacta of Prague, which had been adopted in 1433. The Compacta resolved that both Catholic and Hussite religious observances were equally valid. However, in 1462 Pope Pius II declared that the Compacta was no longer accepted by the Catholic Church and that George of Poděbrady would only be recognized if he complied with the Catholic position.

> GEORGE OF PODĚBRADY HOPED TO CREATE AN ALLIANCE OF CHRISTIAN EUROPEAN REALMS TO COUNTER THE GROWING THREAT OF TURKISH EXPANSION.

George tried to tread a difficult path between ignoring this demand yet placating the Catholic Church by curbing the most radical Hussites. This was not enough for Pope Pius II, nor his successor, Paul II. In 1466, George of Poděbrady was excommunicated and declared deposed by the Pope. The resulting conflict saw Bohemia invaded by neighbouring Hungary. Although the invaders saw some success, they did not take Prague. After the death of George of Poděbrady in 1471, his successor Vladislaus brought the conflict to a successful conclusion, being proclaimed as king of both Hungary and Bohemia.

George of Poděbrady was in many ways a visionary, who saw the possibility of a great alliance of states. However, it is possible to read too much into this. He was not so much trying to create a pan-European super-state as an alliance against the Turks, who had recently conquered Constantinople and threatened to push westwards into Europe. Nevertheless, his idea was ahead of its time and his tolerance of conflicting religious observances unusual in an era of religious conflict and schism.

Successful leadership of the dominant Utraquist faction of the Hussites resulted in George of Poděbrady being proclaimed as king. He was placed in the awkward position of having to challenge some elements of the Hussite movement whilst trying to retain the support of the majority.

IVAN III (THE GREAT) OF RUSSIA (1440–1505)

Father of the Russian state

At the time of Ivan's birth in 1440, Russia still lay under the shadow of the Mongol Empire, the western portion of which was often referred to as the Golden Horde. Large numbers of Turkic tribesmen had been incorporated into the Golden Horde, creating a cultural group generally known in Europe as Tatars.

The Golden Horde was in decline, partly due to the ravages of the Black Death and in part as a result of political

Below: Ivan III's realm fought several wars against the khanate of Kazan, a conflict that continued after his death.

fragmentation. Its independent khanates were still a formidable force, and Russia itself was anything but stable. Ivan's father Vasily, Grand Duke of Moscow, was captured by the Tatars at the Battle of the Kamenka River in 1445, leaving his cousin Dimitri in control of Moscow. Dimitri ransomed Vasily, but made him a prisoner before blinding and exiling him. The young Ivan was handed over to Dimitri, but did not suffer the same fate.

THE REIGN OF IVAN III WAS CHARACTERIZED BY A GRADUAL ACCUMULATION OF TERRITORY, NOT ALL OF IT BY MILITARY MEANS.

Ivan's father was restored to a position of power by Dimitri, probably because he commanded significant support in Moscow, and in time Dimitri was overthrown. Ivan was declared co-ruler with his father at the age of six, and took part in military campaigns on his behalf. By the time he succeeded to the throne in 1462, Ivan had gained control of Moscow's rival Tver by marriage and established himself as a strong war leader.

Ivan's first campaigns were against the Tatars, intending to free Moscow from their control. After clearing this threat from his eastern borders he made war on Novgorod from 1470 onwards. Subduing Novgorod took nearly 20 years, but during this time Ivan was able to negotiate treaties that gave him control of Rostov and Yaroslavl, with Pskov and Ryazan remaining independent in name only. By this time, Ivan's first wife had died. He married Zoe Palaeologus of Byzantium, who changed her name to Sophia.

A successful campaign against the Golden Horde in 1480 enabled Ivan to declare Moscow free of Mongol domination at last, although skirmishing continued for some years. Ivan was assisted in this endeavour by an alliance with the Mongol khan in the Crimea – the Mongol Empire of old was never so divided and would not have permitted differences between its khans to benefit outsiders.

Ivan fought wars against Sweden and

Lithuania, notably taking advantage of a split between Poland and Lithuania. Lithuania's weak position allowed Ivan to gain territory by marriage contract. When the Lithuanians tired of his attempts to annex more of their lands and took up arms, victory at the Vedrosha River in 1500 forced them to cede yet more territory.

Ivan's reign was troubled by rebellion and intrigue, notably a dispute over who was to be his heir. This was brought about by the death from illness of his eldest son in 1490. Ivan was suspicious that there was a plot afoot, and hesitated to name another successor. His eventual choice was his grandson Dimitry, by way of his first marriage to Maria of Tver, which angered his second wife Sophia. Her planned revolt came to nothing, but in 1500 Vasily, his eldest son by Sophia, rebelled and joined the Lithuanian cause. This forced Ivan to make Vasily his heir instead. Most of the intrigue went Ivan's way, however.

IVAN III PURSUED A ROBUST STRATEGY OF CONSOLIDATING HIS POWER BY SEIZING THE TERRITORY OF SUSPECTED TRAITORS AND DISALLOWING INHERITANCES.

Ivan made a practice of taking the lands of any boyar (aristocrat) who was suspected of treason and adding them to his own holdings. He also ruled that princes who had been granted lands as an appanage did not pass them to their descendants; they instead reverted to Ivan. This caused some resentment, but it had the effect of centralizing power.

Ivan the Great died in 1505, leaving behind a powerful legacy. He was the first of the Tsars, having been declared ruler of all Russia in 1479, and established the highly autocratic and centralized system of government that characterized Russian monarchy thereafter. His reign saw Moscow transformed from a city-state to the centre of a Russian state that stretched all the way to the Urals, and for the first time had a clearly defined body of law in a standardized format.

Ivan also adopted the double-headed eagle symbol as a result of his second wife's association with Constantinople, and his efforts to make Moscow a capital fit for his increased status involved major building works including the Kremlin. He also postulated the idea that Moscow was the 'third Rome' (Constantinople being the second) and that there would never be a fourth.

Opposite: Although Ivan III did not personally lead his forces, victory at the Battle of Vedrosha River in 1500 brought to an end Lithuanian resistance to his annexation of territory.

В.К. ІОАННЪ III ВАСИЛЬЕВИЧЪ

Получаетъ извѣстіе о побѣдѣ надъ Литвою,
на берегу рѣки Ведроши, 1500. годъ.

INDEX

PICTURE CREDITS

Alamy: 6 (Classic Image), 8 (Print Collector), 9 (Antiqua Print Gallery), 10 (Granger Collection), 15 (Chronicle), 16 (National Geographic Creative/Tom Lovell), 18 (19th Era), 20 (Prisma Archivo), 21 (Rolf Richardson), 23 (North Wind Picture Archive), 25 (Classic Image), 27 (World History Archive), 28 (Brian Harris), 32 (North Wind Picture Archive), 33 (Interfoto), 35 (World History Archive), 37-39 all (Chronicle), 41 (North Wind Picture Archive), 42 (19th Era), 44 (Niday Picture Library), 46 (Interfoto), 49 (Lordprice Collection), 50 (World History Archive), 53 (Colin Underhill), 54 (Granger Collection), 55 (Chronicle), 60 (19th Era), 61 (Classic Image), 63 (Beryl Peters Collection), 65 (Lebrecht), 66/67 (Art Collection), 68 (Falkensteinfoto), 69 (Chronicle), 70 (Niday Picture Library), 72 (Falkensteinfoto), 73 (Historimages Collection/ Yolanda Perera Sanchez), 74 & 75 (Interfoto), 77 (Historical Image Collection by Bildagentur-online), 78 (Interfoto), 79 (Lanmas), 80 (World History Archive), 81 (Falkensteinphoto), 82 (Archivart), 83 (World History Archive), 84 (Chronicle), 86 (Pictorial Press), 87 (Historical Images Archive), 88 (Timewatch Images), 90 (Science History Images), 91 (Classic Image), 93 (Granger Collection), 96 (Science History Images), 97 (Universal Images Group), 100 (World History Archive), 102 (Pictorial Press), 104 (Photo 12/Archives Snark), 105 (Granger Collection), 108 (Ken Welsh), 110 (Chronicle), 111 (Arte Directors & TRIP/Helene Rogers), 112 (Print Collector), 113 (19th Era), 115 (Classic Image), 116 (World History Archive), 117 (Granger Collection), 119 (Photo 12/ Anne Ronan Picture Library), 120 (Prisma Archivo), 121 (Chronicle), 122 (Photo 12/ Hachede), 123 (Granger Collection), 124 (Ivy Close Images), 126 (Historimages Collection/Yolanda Perera Sanchez), 128 (Florilegius), 129 & 130 (Chronicle), 132 (Florilegius), 133 (Angelo Hornak), 134 (HIP/Historica Graphica Collection), 135 (Photo 12/Archives Snark), 140 (Falkenstein Heinz-Dieter), 141 (Interfoto), 149 (Granger Collection), 150 (Everett Images), 151 (Archive Images), 152/153 (World History Archive), 157 (Masterpics), 158 (Mauritius Images/Steve Vidler), 166 (Imagerbroker), 167 (World History Archive), 168 (Chronicle), 173 (Alamy/Lenmas), 174 (Art Collection 2), 177 (Interfoto), 179 (Historimages/Yolanda Perera Sanchez), 180 (Peter Horree), 181 (Photo 12/Archives Snark), 183 (Chronicle), 184 (Glasshouse Images), 186 (North Wind Picture Archive), 187 (Falkensteinfoto), 198 (PBL Collection), 190 (World History Archive), 191 (G L Archive), 194 (Interfoto), 195 (Chronicle), 196 (Art Collection 4), 198 (World History Archive), 200 (Falkensteinfoto), 201 (Imagebroker), 203 (G L Archive), 205 (Classicpaintings), 209 & 211 (Prisma Archivo), 212 (Classic Image), 216 (Chronicle)

Alamy/Heritage Image Partnership/Fine Art Images: 29, 30/31, 34, 89, 92, 94, 95, 98, 99, 103, 106, 142/143, 145, 146, 154, 156, 165, 206, 214/215, 219

Amber Books: 12 both, 14

Bridgeman Art Library: 137 (Regional Art Museum, Simbirsk)

Depositphotos: 5 & 40 (Phb.cz), 45 & 51 & 57 (Georgios), 76 (Mijeshots), 160/161 (Jorisvo)

Dreamstime: 11 (Colin Young), 193 (Georgios Kollidas)

Mary Evans Picture Library: 136, 148 (Thaliastock)

Getty Images: 58 (UIG/Universal History Archive), 139 (Time Life Pictures), 171 (DEA Picture Library)

Shutterstock: 13 (Marina Kryukova), 85 (Alex Yeung), 159 (A C Jones), 162 (Photo.eccles), 169 & 170 (Jorisvo), 176 (Shyshell)

Pruilegiū regale sup
ry uoie dominis annis. P
tes parit z futuri qz xpt c
hei quez tuio a quibz̃ a̧a
thomia illū tūc prepositū de quo fu
gat ī xpetuio vincliꝰ detinebut
nisi forte elegit par̃ publice a̧